Value-ology

Simon Kelly • Paul Johnston • Stacey Danheiser

Value-ology

Aligning sales and marketing to shape and deliver
profitable customer value propositions

Simon Kelly
Rotherham, South Yorkshire,
United Kingdom

Stacey Danheiser
Denver, Colorado, USA

Paul Johnston
Nottingham, Nottinghamshire,
United Kingdom

ISBN 978-3-319-45625-6   ISBN 978-3-319-45626-3   (eBook)
DOI 10.1007/978-3-319-45626-3

Library of Congress Control Number: 2016961069

Infinity set Creative RF By: khalus Getty Images 165900411

Printed on acid-free paper

This Palgrave Macmillan imprint is published by Springer Nature
The registered company is Springer International Publishing AG
The registered company address is: Gewerbestrasse 11, 6330 Cham, Switzerland

Preface

Today, 52% of the companies that were in the Fortune 500 in 2000 are no longer on the list. They fell off because of bankruptcy, mergers and acquisitions or because they were replaced by better-performing companies. As competition and innovation rapidly heat up, what is your organisation doing to survive or thrive? In this book we focus on the single biggest contributor to the success or failure of companies: staying in tune with what your customers value.

Without competitively differentiated and resonating value propositions, your firm will die. Without alignment between sales, marketing and customers, your firm will die. Bob Garrat, in his book *The Fish Rots From The Head*, describes the death of companies that fail to learn about markets, customers and themselves as 'often slow and grisly'.

To survive and thrive we argue that it's time to go back to the basics by putting a focus on creating value for your customers. Over the past two decades, we've seen first hand what can be accomplished when sales and marketing work together to understand and deliver customer value.

On the one hand, company marketing departments are producing more and more content than ever before. It would seem that much of this is ineffective as customers get bombarded, in their ever-crowded inboxes, with irrelevant material. Companies are creating a lot of noise, but failing to resonate with their customers. In fact, according to Corporate Executive Board (CEB) research, 94% of prospects have completely disengaged with vendors because their content fails to resonate, to put it politely. Despite the lack of effectiveness, marketers continue to waste millions of dollars on creating irrelevant messages and tools, unaware that the consequence is customer detachment.

This is happening at a time when, more than ever, it has become imperative to produce good marketing content. In this omni-channel era, where potential buyers get lots of product and company information online, 67 % of buyers have a clear picture of the solution they want before they engage a sales rep (Sirius Decisions 2014). CEB research showed that business-to-business buyers tend to be over 60 % of the way through the sales process before they contact a salesperson. It seems that if you fail to talk to customers about the things that are important to them, based on what they see as relevant value, they will have checked out of your electronic building before your sales rep gets in to see them.

On the other hand, we're witnessing a shift in how organisations are making purchasing decisions. Coming out of the recession towards the end of the first decade of this millennium, many organisations appreciated more than ever how volatile financial and economic conditions could threaten the very existence of their businesses. As a result they continued to keep a cautious attitude towards how corporate budgets were spent and how buying decisions were made. This financially prudent mind-set has resulted in an increasingly 'conservative consensus seeking' approach to purchasing. Now, more departments are involved and there is far less likely to be one central decision-maker, but rather a full team or committee. CEB research estimates that on average 5.4 people are involved in decision-making for a significant purchase. This means a greater opportunity for the deal to fall apart if all parties aren't involved in the process and bought in.

According to Qvidian (Sales Execution Trends 2014), 58 % of deals end up in 'no decision' because sales has not presented value effectively. We believe this number will continue to rise until organisations put in place a formal programme to continuously capture customer intelligence and insights and connect the dots for their prospects on how their organisation can uniquely solve their challenges.

There is ample evidence that the sunny uplands are worth striving for, as 91 % (CEB study cited in Pisello 2015) of executives said they would happily forward marketing content if they found it insightful and relevant. Aberdeen Group found that companies who leverage online resources to increase their customer understanding typically grew by over 21 %. Research by Professor Malcolm McDonald at Cranfield University, a leading UK business school, showed that developing a customer value-led approach could lead to at least a 10 % growth in revenue. We have seen similar uplifts in performance where we have helped companies implement the approach outlined in this book.

If you cannot resonate with the customer by tapping into what they value then you're left racing to the bottom on price. We know that a 5 % price reduction typically leads to a 16% drop in profitability. So what's it to be: a 10% plus growth in revenue or a 16% plus drop in profitability? Money wasted on irrelevant customer content or invested in resonating value propositions that drive growth?

You may be wondering what's different and better about this book compared with others you may have seen or read. Well, some of the others give you simple models that allow you to start internally 'crowd storming' your value propositions. This is fine in and of itself but fails to take into account the complexity that's involved in understanding customer value, getting buy-in to this approach inside your organisation and, crucially, getting alignment between the customer, marketing and sales. All of this together is what makes up 'value-ology', a mix of objective analysis and creative insight. We'd like to think that this book is for 'thoughtful practitioners' who want to understand the what and why questions before jumping straight to how. We know that people within companies can differ widely about what they perceive as value. Jumping straight to 'crowd storming' the how can be short-term fun, quickly followed by failure. As Peter Senge in his book *The Fifth Discipline* says, proactivity is often just reactivity in disguise, and typically lacks a well-thought-through basis for action.

We've seen many books that are unashamedly about promoting a sexy new piece of research with a claim that the next new thing has been discovered. Here, there's a tendency to ignore all that has gone before. Hopefully you can see, right off the bat, in this short introduction that we've brought together highly reputable academic and commercial research from other authors and organisations. We've supplemented this with three pieces of original research that we have carried out ourselves. In using this 'mixed methods' approach, we're eating our own dog food, as this is the method we recommend you take for developing a value-based approach. Crucially, we provide an overall set of insights based on the best research available. Unashamedly we present research by CEB, Sirius Decisions and other credible organisations and add our own to it. Uniquely we use the best of academic input, mostly ignored by many commercial marketing practices, to add to the weight and credibility of our insights.

We know that some of you are looking for help with the 'how to', so we provide you with frameworks and specific action steps. These will help you create value across the entire marketing and sales value chain, to keep and grow existing customers, gain new customers and continue to create value for future purchases. Before we get to the how to in each chapter, we seek to help you improve your understanding of concepts and issues that will help you successfully drive a customer value-led approach into your business, developing your value-ology. Importantly, we help you make the business case for this approach by providing lots of credible supporting data and insights.

What often gets ignored is the problems organisations seem to have in gaining alignment between sales and marketing. This book will help you understand what the issues are here and set you on a path to align marketing and sales together with the most important stakeholder—the customer. We believe that in order to grow fast, sales and marketing teams need to grow up and align. They need to work together to truly understand their customers' needs, wants, motivations and pain points so that they can offer compelling value. We offer an approach that takes you soup to nuts—from developing value propositions through to executing effective campaigns and communications, with lots more in between.

The book is based on our combined academic, corporate and consultancy experience. We've worked with marketing and sales teams of all sizes across dozens of industries. We've also surveyed and interviewed over 200 senior marketing and sales executives across the globe to get their input. We've successfully executed this approach inside organisations we've worked in and with companies we've worked for on assignments. Value-ology will teach you how to guarantee that the marketing content you produce and the sales conversations you deliver to potential customers produce profitable results.

It will help you understand that different people and organisations come from different places. This will help you navigate, communicate and motivate your organisation to adopt a value-based approach.

Good luck in your quest for value-ology.

Value-ology recognises that the quest to unlock customer value is a combination of objective analysis to unearth customer value, creative insight to tap into customer value, development of value propositions that resonate with customers, effective sales and marketing alignment, consistent execution and feedback mechanisms to improve value offerings.

Acknowledgements

We would like to thank all those who made time available and offered their support, input, ideas and remarks throughout this book writing journey. Your stories inspired us and helped bring this book to life.

To all of the brilliant research firms for publishing reputable data about the state of our industry. To the many exceptional marketing and sales leaders who have guided and motivated us throughout the years. And to the authors whose works provoked us to write. We thank you all.

Most importantly, we express our sincere gratitude to our spouses and families for their encouragement and understanding as we worked through the creative process.

Thank you to Palgrave Macmillan for allowing us to publish this book.

Last and not least, to our former, current and future students for your willingness to learn new concepts and approaches.

Foreword

"So many people can't answer the "what" and "why" questions and then head off on the "how" path wasting corporate resources and customer calories…I won't let people talk to me about the "how" until we are grounded with confidence on the "what and why"…

Andrew Crouch, President, EMEA, Level 3 Communications

My own research confirms the findings of McKinsey that all organisations talk about quantified value propositions, but only 5% have them. In 2016 and after well over 100 years of marketing, this is a disgraceful state of affairs and reflects very badly on our discipline.

So I began a search to discover what has been written about this crucial topic and was extremely disappointed with what I found.

For a start, the word "value" itself is widely misunderstood, whilst processes for understanding and developing value propositions do not appear to exist. Furthermore, virtually no scholarly research has been done on the elusive issue of organisational value co-creation.

Given that differentiation today is more challenging than at any time in our history and that it lies at the very heart of marketing, it seems logical to me that, unless an organisation can demonstrate how dealing with them will create advantage for the customer, it will have no option but to move inexorably towards being a commodity supplier.

It is, therefore, with great pleasure that I came across the manuscript for this book, which is not only easy to read and underpinned by research, but is highly pragmatic and is a major step forward in filling the void in the domain of creating value for customers.

I personally have been looking forward to a book like this for a number of years and congratulate the authors on what I believe is a major contribution to marketing.

Professor Malcolm McDonald, MA (Oxon), MSc, PhD, DLitt, DSc
Emeritus Professor
Cranfield School of Management, Cranfield University

Value-ology

VALUE-OLOGY: Aligning sales and marketing to shape and deliver profitable customer value.

"A unique insight into understanding, developing and articulating customer value propositions that work in sales conversations and through marketing channels. Mobilising marketing and sales to work together to create value for the customer can deliver great results; I can vouch for that."

Andrew Crouch, President, EMEA, Level 3 Communications

"The more you understand your customers the clearer things become. The key to building a great customer experience is to understand how customer value creating value propositions improve their lives. I've witnessed this approach in action and seen it deliver powerful results. Highly recommended reading."

Colin Shaw, CEO, Beyond Philosophy, and award-winning author

"Easy to read, underpinned by research, and highly pragmatic. This is a major step forward in filling the void in the domain of creating value for customers."

Professor Malcolm McDonald, Emeritus Professor,
Cranfield School of Management, Cranfield University

"About 20 years ago Flash had an advertising line 'we do the hard work so you don't have to'. Well clearly no book could be a substitute for hard work but it could be something that would really help you practically to deliver tangible improvements in customer value. Don't make mistakes you don't have to when the very wise authors have pulled together all this research and knowledge and put it at your fingertips."

Amanda Mackenzie, OBE, Chief Executive, Business in the Community

"Top performing companies have one thing in common – they understand who their customers are and what they care about most. This book provides a practical, step-by-step guide to uncover and articulate customer value. A book foundational to delivering on customer value and to your business success."

Tony Zambito, Founder, Buyer Personas

"Moving customer conversations from product to customer value sounds simple, but it's not easy. Managing your sales and marketing assets in this way creates lasting competitive advantage because it is not easy to replicate. I have experienced the kind of growth the value-ology approach can help drive. This book can help you mobilise customer value in your own organisation. Highly recommended. A winning approach!"

Danny McLaughlin, former Managing Director, BT Major Business

Contents

About the Authors

Stacey Danheiser is co-founder of SHAKE Marketing Group, based in Denver, Colorado, where she works with B2B clients to implement integrated marketing strategies and teach them about customer-centricity. Prior to starting her own consultancy, she spent 15 years as a marketing and sales enablement leader at large firms across cable, telecom, financial services and banking sectors.

Paul Johnston joined Sheffield Business School (part of Sheffield Hallam University) over ten years ago. Prior to this, he spent 20 years in the gambling and electronic games industry. He served on the boards of several companies in competitive strategy, research and product innovation roles. Paul has recently been involved with a customer centric services module of the Sheffield City Leadership Programme and a range of large corporate projects, as well as undergraduate and postgraduate student tutoring.

Simon Kelly has 35 years' experience in the ICT industry in customer service, sales and marketing. He was Marketing Director for BT Major Business, where he pioneered the move from 'product push' to 'value-based' selling and marketing. He led a canon of knowledge for the CIM on best practice B2B marketing. Now a 'pracademic', he has developed innovative marketing and sales skills modules for Sheffield Business School where he is a Senior Lecturer. He is co-founder of SHAKE Marketing Group, based in London.

List of Figures

Part 1

Building the Foundation of Value-ology

1

What Is Value?

In this chapter we will look at:

- Bringing the value conversation into the open
- Defining value
- Understanding different types of value
- A word on value and values
- The dynamic nature of value
- Mapping your value perspective

The Elephant in the Room

As businesspeople, we know that marketing is an activity that helps a company to make money by achieving sustained competitive advantage. It does this by knowing what the customer needs and making sure the business gives it to them in a way that is different from and better than competing offers. Many sales and marketing professionals have received training and education in colleges and universities and have become familiar with the *classic* marketing management tools of business analysis and decision-making, such as customer segmentation, targeting and positioning, and how to manage the marketing mix.

Right at the heart of sales and marketing practice lies the concept of 'value'. Yet pick up a typical marketing or sales management textbook and it is barely mentioned. It's as if the idea of value is so self-evident that it hardly warrants

© The Author(s) 2017
S. Kelly et al., *Value-ology*,
DOI 10.1007/978-3-319-45626-3_1

further discussion. We all know what it is, we all know how to create it, we all know how to deliver it and we all know how to communicate it.] And that's exactly where a company's problems on the subject of value can begin because value is the elephant in the room. Something big and obvious that we all know we should pay more attention to really understanding, yet choose not to do so.

Here is an example to show you what we mean. We can remember being part of a meeting with one of the largest licensed hospitality retailers in the UK. This company owned a large chain of pubs and they were very keen to improve the image and experience of pub visiting in order to attract women and families. The retailer's representative (who had significant influence over how many products were placed) opened the conversation with 'we are all about giving our customers value for money'. Everyone in the room naturally agreed, and soon everyone in the industry was coming up with product developments that they believed delivered 'value for money'. The thing was, everyone interpreted what the customer and customer's customer wanted differently, and large amounts of time were devoted to debating the merits of new product concepts without ever establishing what 'value for money' really meant and for whom. For some, it was increased revenue for the pub owner, for some it was increased consumer dwell time in the pub, for others it meant designing less male-oriented products, and so on.

Everyone, it seemed, had a different point of view about how value for money could be delivered, and overlooked the fact that they hadn't made it clear what was meant by value in the first place.

Why Is Getting a Common View on Value Difficult?

The challenge of coming to a common understanding of what value looks like lies deeper than just solving the everyday communication problem of making sure people in the organisation talk to each other and share the information they have about what customers need, what their attitudes and behaviours are and how they make buying decisions.

Simply collecting every last detail about the customer doesn't necessarily lead to a better understanding of what makes them tick. This is because the people we work with often have different views about the most significant aspect of the value conversation. What is seen as important to one person might be ignored by another. This happens because we are selective in the way we process information: we tend to pay attention to information that confirms our world view and reject information that challenges it. Furthermore, experienced executives can fall prey to what Ron Westrum of Eastern Michigan University in his article 'Social intelligence about hidden events: Its significance for scientific research and social policy' called 'the fallacy of centrality'. This is where individuals such as seasoned sales and marketing professionals are convinced they know everything that is going on in their market sector and with their customers, so they treat anything new or unusual as completely implausible and deny it matters to the business. In other words, if they don't know about it, how can it possibly be true?

Therefore people in different roles and at different levels have diverse views about value. The chief financial officer (CFO) might only pay attention to what the customer has to say about price because his/her world revolves around finance, whereas the key account manager might place particular importance on information sharing and idea creation because his/her world revolves around customer service. Alternatively, the chief marketing officer (CMO), who has been head of the department for several years, disregards input from a junior sales executive when s/he reports back that customers are saying the basis of the present market offering is off target because customers are saying they place more value on access to the supplier's business network rather than the future proofing of products promoted in the current marketing campaign. Value for each individual is regarded as such a self-evident thing they don't spend time thinking too deeply about it and they don't expect their co-workers to have a significantly different take from their own.

Organisational psychologist Chris Argyris has studied how professionals avoid thinking deeply about the assumptions they have about their business world and how it works. In his book *On Organisational Learning* he says we take our assumptions for granted and fail to realise the powerful influence they have on the way we interpret information, make decisions and take action. This means we have to put extra time, thought and energy into bringing these taken-for-granted assumptions to the surface if we are to solve the puzzle of what customer value really means. It needs to done before we even start to discuss our personal ideas on how to deliver and communicate value, otherwise we might jump to conclusions and get locked into a cycle of talking past each other in the value conversation.

This means that before anything else we need to establish *what* we are talking about. Doing this is not as easy as it seems. Organisations are places where personal reputations, power and ambitions reside. Argyris tells us that because of this we engage in defensive reasoning to protect our positions and our egos. Therefore, in the case of something as profound as the question 'so what do you actually mean by value' people feel too embarrassed to ask or too fearful to challenge what is meant by it. The situation gets progressively worse over time as the topic is swept under the carpet or, as Argyris says, it becomes 'undiscussable'. It gets worse still when it becomes accepted as a cultural norm that 'we don't talk about what we mean by value around here', which means that even mentioning there might be an issue to resolve becomes undiscussable too!

Of course, many companies are very good at researching what customers value. They spend a lot of time and money forecasting trends, doing market research and speaking with customers to find out what matters to the buyer and the consumer in order to understand the benefits they seek and what they need. This is the everyday pursuit of value understanding, and so you might expect that most companies have a consistent and commonly understood view of what value means in their sector and for their customers.

The challenge comes when customers need change, when there are competing versions of what value is, such as the marketing perspective and the sales perspective, because organisations are large and complex, or the value conversation never takes place at all.

The Ambiguity of What Is Meant by Value

Back in 1997 McKinsey consultants Ralf Leszinski and Mike Marn wrote in their article 'Setting the value not the price' that:

> Value may be one of the most overused and misused terms in marketing and pricing.

The term value is powerful. Who would seriously challenge the common sense of the corporate rallying cry to 'deliver better customer value'? As we have noted above, the problem arises when the customer and the supplier, different departments and different people have different ideas about what value is. And the problem is compounded when people don't share their assumptions about it.

Nikolas Tzokas and Michael Saren from Strathclyde University in Scotland bring home the point when they observed, in their *Australian Marketing Journal* article titled 'Value transformation in relationship marketing', that:

> the value concept has become a flagship of every constituency of the firm and any contemporary organisation as a whole.

Everyone it seems has hold of a different part of the value elephant and wears a cognitive blindfold so they can't see what part others are holding and how it differs from theirs. It stands to reason, therefore, that unless everyone in the business understands the complexities and subtleties that make up value it will be impossible to successfully manage the drivers and facilitators of value that the business needs.

Value Defined

Commercial interest in the idea of value is nothing new. Ever since people began trading vegetables for meat, they have been interested in value. Christian Gronroos, in his 1996 article 'Relationship marketing: Strategic and tactical implications', explained that the ancient rice traders of China were very aware of relationship value. Tim Ambler, in his 2006 chapter of Vargo and Lusch's *The Service Dominant Logic of Marketing*, titled 'The new dominant logic of marketing: Views of the elephant', describes how the merchants of the Middle Ages balanced function, scarcity and perception of goods with a so called *just price*. Businesspeople have always negotiated value.

With value being such a slippery idea, it's no wonder that university professors and businesspeople have had a tough time coming up with a definition that everyone agrees with. Over the years several definitions have been suggested.

Azzadin Salem Khalifa, Associate Professor of Strategic Management, University of Sharjah UAE, in his article 'Customer value: A review of recent literature and an integrative configuration', defines it as:

> not what the producer puts in, but what the customer gets out.

In their article 'Customer value assessment in business markets: A state-of-practice study', James Anderson, William L. Ford Distinguished Professor of Marketing and Wholesale Distribution North Western University, Pradeep Chintagunta, Associate Professor of Marketing, J.L. Kellogg Graduate North Western University, and Dipak Jain, Assistant Professor of Marketing, S.C. Johnson Graduate School of Management, Cornell University, suggest:

> Value in business markets [is] the perceived worth in monetary units of the set of economic, technical, service and social benefits received by a customer firm in exchange for the price paid for a product, taking into consideration the available suppliers' offerings and prices.

In his frequently cited seminal article 'Customer value: The next source for competitive advantage', Robert Woodruff, Emeritus Professor of Marketing at the University of Tennessee, says:

> Customer value is a customer's perceived preference for and evaluation of those product attributes, attribute performances, and consequences arising from use that facilitate (or block) achieving the customer's goals and purposes in use situations.

Morris Holbrook, Professor of Marketing at The Graduate School of Business, Columbia University, in his book *Consumer Value: A Framework for Analysis and Research*, defines value as:

> an interactive relativistic preference experience

Michael Porter, Bishop William Lawrence University Professor, Harvard Business School, in his book *Competitive Strategy. Techniques for Analysing Industries and Competitors*, describes value as:

> the price someone is willing to pay

The workable definition we will be using throughout this book is:

Value = perceived *relevant and distinct* benefit − total cost of ownership

Different Types of Value

Where you sit affects what you see. Unless you're wearing a blindfold, of course! This means that you will see things differently depending on what you think matters. Economists, financiers and accountants emphasise monetary value, customer psychologists pay attention to perceived value, relationship marketers single out relationship value, service marketers zone in on experiential value, people concerned with corporate social responsibility talk about social value and business professors study the conceptual difference between exchange value and use value.

Whilst all these aspects of value are frequently looked at individually, it seems sensible to bear in mind that they are interrelated. Some people have their particular favourite, and so when they talk about value they champion the assumptions of their preferred perspective and play down the others. The scope for disagreement, talking at cross-purposes and misunderstanding between co-workers is huge.

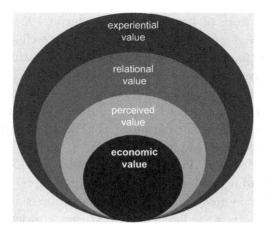

Fig. 1.1 The value onion

The different dimensions can be thought of as layers of an onion. Each layer is different, and at the same time they all relate together in a whole. The *value onion* above shows the core is the transactional and functional dimension of economic value and the outer layers the less tangible dimensions of value that relate to immediate perceptions, the processes and exchanges of relationship value, and the extensive and subtle aspects of social and experiential value (Fig. 1.1).

Economic Value

The focus of economic value is concerned with the cost of a transaction. Something is deemed to be better value if the same or similar products are obtained for less money than the alternatives. For that reason it is the most fundamental aspect of thinking about value and exchange of goods, services and money. There can be no escaping the fact that cost and profit matter to the customer and the supplier. It is this view of value that is commonly seen in the consumer retail sector, where 'great value' is often synonymous with a cheaper price.

Perceived Value

The idea that customers perceive value in different ways has been recognised by scholars and businesspeople for a long time. Some of the earliest formal attempts to define perceived value have their roots in the value analysis and value engineering work of Lawrence Miles, who in 1961 said in his book *Techniques of Value Analysis and Engineering* that as well as monetary value factors customers talked of value in terms of perceived usefulness of a product and the sense of personal esteem they got from being seen to purchase and use it. This was built on by Griffen and Hauser, and their approach to capturing the 'voice of the customer' which was outlined in their 1993 *Marketing Science* article 'The voice of the customer' as a way of ensuring the customer perspective was recognised in product designs.

It was Valerie Zeithaml, Professor of Marketing at UNC Kenan Flagler Business School, who developed this line of thinking by using the idea of 'give and get'. She pointed out that of course customers are concerned with cost and usefulness, but the key issue is that each customer has a different perception of what they *give* for what they *get*. What this means is that value is not a constant, objective, monetary calculation, because it changes depending on how the customer perceives the sacrifices he/she is making (such as time, money, hassle) and how the offer is perceived relative to the competition.

In the field of consumer marketing Morris Holbrook identified eight types of value that he divided into four extrinsic and four intrinsic dimensions. These spanned a full range of value types from direct utility value through to symbolic value.

8 Types of Value

- Efficiency
- Excellence
- Status
- Esteem
- Play
- Aesthetics
- Ethics
- Spirituality (how much the solution gives meaning to someone's life)

Holbrook reinforces the argument that value is relative to individuals across these dimensions, and whilst it was originally focused on consumers, academics such as Patricia Coutelle-Brillet, Arnaud Riviere and Veronique des Garets believe this work is relevant to business customers too. For example the sense of status and esteem in the eyes of others that industrial buyers get when they use well-known supplier brands is a recognised phenomenon that indicates their professionalism as a means to impress colleagues and competitors and as a way to manage the fear, uncertainty and doubt of supply chain management. As they used to say, 'nobody got sacked for buying IBM'.

The idea of perceived value explains why defining value is such a tricky thing to do. Value refers to a range of tangible and intangible customer considerations. In particular it is subjective, it can change over time, it can change owing to circumstances and situation. In the end value is a <u>highly personal</u> and idiosyncratic <u>judgement</u>.

Relational Value

An important development of customer-perceived value is the idea of relationship value. This is primarily concerned with the intangible aspects of value that occur between people and is especially important in business-to-business (B2B) customer relationships. Relational value is often associated with the *service* that firms give their customers, and yet the creation of relational and service value is not easily pinned down. In 2012 Christian Gronroos remarked in his article 'Conceptualising value co-creation: A journey to the 1970s and back to the future' that relational value creation was:

> one of the most ill-defined and elusively used concepts in service marketing

There are several things that it is important to consider in the context of relationship value.

- Doing business is not a single transaction, several exchanges occur over time
- The relationship itself adds value to the core solution offered
- Value can be both added and subtracted during the course of a relationship
- Value is mutually created for both supplier and customer

Thinking about relationship value shifts the focus attention away from price and product attributes alone, and gets us thinking about the way customer interactions take place over time and the wider network of stakeholders who are engaged in the purchase of a product. It is especially the case in B2B interactions that several people come together as the decision making unit.

> value for the customer is not embedded in transactional exchange of a product for money. Instead customer perceived value is created and delivered over time as the relationship develops.

So wrote Professor Christian Gronross, Professor of Marketing, and Annika Ravald, post-doctoral researcher at the Hanken School of Economics, in 'The value concept and relationship marketing', *European Journal of Marketing*, 30, No. 2 (1996), pp. 19–30.

Relational value in a B2B context has been the subject of particular study by Professor Wolfgang Ulaga, who identified eight key relational value elements:

- Product quality
- Delivery
- Time to market
- Direct costs (compared with competition and frequency of price increases)
- Service support
- Supplier know-how
- Personal interaction
- Process costs

In his article 'Capturing value creation in business relationships: A customer perspective' Professor Ulaga points out that whilst these dimensions are related to create an overall impression of value, they are not directly linked together in terms of cause and effect. This means that suppliers can continue to have strong sales by providing excellent product quality whilst at the same time giving poor service. It is therfore the overall sense of relational value in a B2B situation that needs to be considered.

Taking a closer look at the ways in which value can be added and subtracted over time, researchers have identified several factors.

Things That Add Relationship Value Include

The use of specialised knowledge skills and competence, the development of trust, showing commitment and feeling at ease, commercial attractiveness through access to wider networks of suppliers, customers and influencers, competence in managing supplier–customer relationships through effective communication, dialogue and problem resolution.

Things That Subtract Relationship Value Include

Unhelpful staff, difficult to navigate spaces and processes, incompetence, lateness, inconsistency, unfulfilled promises, rudeness, aggression, mendacity.

From the relational value perspective the idea of mutuality between the supplier and the customer is seen as very significant. What this means is that the supplier and the customer create and derive value simultaneously through-out the relationship. This can be thought of as a win/win situation. Crucially this perspective signals a very different way of thinking about value, because value isn't just added to the offer and then sold to the customer; it is actually produced as the relationship happens. Nikolaos Tzokas and Mike Saren called this aspect of relationship value creation the 'co-production of value', where customers and suppliers work closely together to create optimal solutions.

Experiential Value

Experiential value refers to the sense of value a customer gets from the whole experience of dealing with a supplier. In its simplest form it can be thought of in terms of how pleasant, exciting, supportive and competent the B2B experience is.

A more sophisticated way of thinking about experiential value extends the idea of relationship to a concern with the well-being of the whole network and system of business, customer and societal interactions. This view lies at the heart of the work of Stephen Vargo and Robert Lusch called *Service Dominant Logic*. One of the big ideas in this approach that has reached main-stream management is the idea of the *co-creation of value*. In 2008 Stephen Vargo, Paul Maglio and Melissa Akaka explained in their article 'On value and value co-creation: A service systems and service logic perspective' how there are two main ways of looking at value and value creation. These are *value in exchange* and *value in use*. It is in the value in use perspective where the co-creation of value resides.

Value in exchange is the way we conventionally talk about value creation. Common sense tells us that value is created by companies in the products and services they provide, and this is then distributed and sold to markets. Suppliers and customers are two separate entities in a supply chain. A phar-maceutical company puts value into its products by transforming basic mate-rials into medicines that benefit the customer. This valuable product is then exchanged for money. This is also known as a *goods dominant logic* because value is seen to be embedded in the goods being sold. Seems pretty obvious, doesn't it? However, this point of view is based on some taken-for-granted assumptions about how value is created.

Value in use is a challenge to this deeply ingrained assumption about value creation. Using *service dominant* logic the supplier and the customer are not separate entities in which value is passed from supplier to the cus-tomer. Suppliers and customer are imagined as part of a value creating system where value is created jointly and reciprocally and both parties need to pay attention to the health of the whole commercial relationship and the market sector they operate in, not just to their own needs. Thinking about the pharmaceutical company again, the firm uses its internal resources and human competences to change raw materials into medicines. These medicines have no value until they are consumed and take effect; they don't have any value sitting on a shelf in the medicine cupboard. The value created comes from a wider value network than just the one-off purchase of the good. The medicines are also integrated with other resources such as the skill and knowledge of doctors and nurses, medical facilities and even caring parents and teachers. The medicine only has value when it is used in the context of the life of the customer. At the same time the supplier also obtains financial value and reputational value not only for making people feel better but also for ethical production of the medicines and improving the welfare of society as a whole.

The idea of value in use prompts us to consider two further things. Firstly the principle of *customer participation* in the development of products and services, rather than customers simply being market research informants (people to be researched rather than included), and secondly the appreciation of *value appropriation*, which emphasises the need for the supplier to obtain value from the exchange as well. The idea of value appropriation cautions organisations against running away with the idea of an obsession with customer centricity alone. Something that Professor Evert Gummesson in his 2008 article 'Customer centricity: Reality or wild goose chase' called an unbalanced wild goose chase, where the supplier organisation simply ends up reacting to every customer whim to the detriment of the business. Customer centricity is yet another everyday taken-for-granted assumption that frequently goes unchallenged because the principles of marketing are now so deeply embedded in the management psyche.

Supported by our research, we believe that B2B sales professionals instinctively think in terms of *value in use* rather than *value in exchange*, and as such it is a fundamental point of view that forms the basis of a different view of value to their colleagues in other departments and functions.

Social Value

Social value takes the idea of a value ecosystem to its furthest extent. Fundamentally it is a challenge to the ideas of Milton Friedman, who said that the primary and exclusive concern of a firm is the creation of value for shareholders. This economic view of value has been recently challenged even by the esteemed economist Professor Michael Porter in an article in *Harvard Business Review* titled 'Creating shared value'.

The main line of his argument is that unfettered self-interested capitalism, consumerism and materialism are bad for the whole system of economy and society. The so-called *hardnosed* approach to business needs to be balanced with a very clear sense of corporate social responsibility. This is not just some fluffy rhetorical feel-good initiative; it's good for business too. As Porter says:

> societal needs not just conventional economic needs, define markets, and social harms can create internal costs for firms

This cutting-edge way of thinking about value is affecting some of the biggest companies on the planet. Satya Nadella, Microsoft's CEO, has recently proclaimed that the company isn't entirely focused on cash and profit these days.

Buyer Myopia and Value Destruction

The unintended consequences of taking an exclusively economic view of value is described by David Farmer (1997), in the *European Journal of Purchasing and Supply Management*, as Purchaser Myopia. This idea refers to a short-term fixation with cost to the exclusion of all other considerations. Perceived, relational and experiential value are ignored, and all that matters to the professional buyer is the cheapest price.

We recall the example of a buyer of integrated circuits who worked for a electronic games manufacturer. He believed he could purchase an apparently identical product from a new supplier at a better price. He didn't consult with the design engineers, and whilst broadly compatible the integrated circuit was not as reliable, lacked certain facilities and created problems in terms of continuity of supply and quality assurance. Furthermore, the long-term relationship with the incumbent supplier was fractured, and almost irrevocably lost, as confidential idea-sharing and joint problem-solving ceased.

The idea of value destruction relates primarily to the supplier and occurs through dysfunctional behaviours, such as rudeness, lack of attention and so on. However, value can also be destroyed if the customer is deliberately awkward and disengaged.

Of course money matters, and so we shouldn't run away with the idea that value is all about image, experience and relational warmth factors. But at the same time we don't think it's just about economic impact. An optimal balance needs to be achieved that is appropriate to the customer and the market sector, even to the extent of the supplier being candid about whether a particular customer is desirable as an account. Not all customers are good to do business with, as unthinkingly buying into the idea of customer centricity might lead you to believe.

The Difference Between Quality, Satisfaction and Value

Robert Woodruff explains that one of the problems of talking about value is that it is often used with other hard-to-define terms such as utility, worth quality, satisfaction and benefits.

As we know customer satisfaction is a very common and worthwhile measure of marketing effectiveness. However, satisfaction can only be measured after the customer has used or experienced the solution. Measuring the satisfaction you get from something is always post hoc.

Value, on the other hand, is different and can be assessed before, during and after the use of the solution. This is especially important for the idea of value proposition, which we will talk about later. The value of the proposition can be anticipated and judged by the customer in advance, and the value of relationship is being continually assessed from the moment of the very first customer encounter.

It's the same for quality. Although it's tempting to assume that quality and value are interchangeable terms, again they refer to different things. Valerie Zeithaml distinguishes value from quality by suggesting quality is the objective assessment of technical product and service features whereas value is an overall subjective judgement of a product or service. So we can see that the value conversation makes us much more aware of a broad range of factors that are considered by customers in the round, from the tangible aspects of the core offer through to the subjective impressions of service and experience.

A Word on Value, Values

Value and values are two closely related but very distinct topics that are commonly discussed in association with the creation of customer value. Making the distinction is important if we want to achieve a clearer understanding of what we mean when we talk about customer value.

['Values' are lasting deeply held personal beliefs typically relating to what we think is important in life, such as freedom, justice and morality.]We apply a value judgement to these values which indicates their worth to ourselves as individuals. For some people morality might be valued more than freedom, which means that they believe society needs clear and firm moral standards that restrict people from behaving in any way they wish. In the business world values often refer to respect, integrity and open communication. Jim Collins and Jerry Porras, authors of the book *Built to Last*, refer to these values as core values:

(a small set of timeless guiding principles that require no external justification)

One trap that organisations can fall into is when they promote and sell their personal and organisational values 'as if' it is directly the value the customer wants from a particular solution. Take the case of Walt Disney, for example. One of their core values is 'a fanatical attention to detail and consistency'. (Whilst this underpins the way they go about business, the customer is more concerned with the benefit that these values deliver in practice.) Let's say some parents take their kids to the cinema to watch *Frozen* in order to spend family time together, be entertained and be part of a global phenomenon. Unless they are a family of cinematography geeks they don't go explicitly to marvel at the detail and consistency of the film's creation; they just want great family time and happy kids.

Similarly a police organisation in South Yorkshire in the UK was rightly proud of its organisational values of trust, responsiveness and diversity, and promoted them vigorously as something it believed mattered to the community. But while these were celebrated internal values, they were quite different from the community's expressed need to feel safe, deter crime and catch criminals. It's a mistake to presume that the values of your organisation are what the customer wants to buy. Of course organisational and personal values shape the way business is done, and might well be something that is valued by the customer as an aspect of relational and experiential value. The key thing to remember, though, is that values are determined by company directors, executives and co-workers, whereas customer value is only ever determined by the customer.

Just to be clear. Understanding customers' deeply held beliefs (their values) is an important part of understanding customer value and forms aspects of their perceived and experiential value sets. In particular customer values are embedded in their sense of identity and self-expression, and link to their choice of brand and supplier. It is the interplay of value and values that is studied in fields such consumer culture theory and the understanding of the symbolic value of products and brands and *goodness* of things and people (see Levy 1959; Ng and Smith 2012; Karababa and Kjelgaard 2014).

The Dynamic Nature of Value

One of the dangers of believing that there is one enduring and absolute definition of value in your business is that there will be times where your prior understanding is irrelevant to the situation you find yourself in.

The circumstances customers find themselves in are always changing. They may have to respond to a competitor, a short term production crisis or a financial circumstance that causes the company to favour short- or long-term perspectives. They may wish to reposition their brand, reinvigorate their innovation capability or expand into new markets.

Whatever the reason, there is no guarantee that what was regarded as good value yesterday will be seen as good value today. Today value is the best price, tomorrow it's product customisation. An example of this from our own experience was when one us had a damaged house door. The initial replacement considerations were aesthetic: making sure the door was the right style for the house and the neighbourhood. Sourcing this customised door took longer than expected, and whilst waiting for it there was an attempted burglary on the home. The priority shifted urgently from aesthetics to home security. This type of value shift occurs all the time in B2B sales, to the extent where we know of examples where customers have to pay a premium to get a larger allocation of a limited production supply.

So the next time someone in your company starts talking about ideas of value for money or the idea of 'value added', which has been popularised in trade publications and consultancy books, be sure to deeply understand the sort of value for money they are talking about or the sort of value supposedly being added.

Value is a multi-faceted moving target. It varies by customer, even within the same sector. It varies by circumstance and it varies by personal interpretation of the buyer. Let's give the final word to Robert Vargo and Stephen Lusch who in their article 'Service-dominant logic: Continuing the evolution' invite us to always treat value as:

Idiosyncratic, experiential, contextual and meaning laden.

In summary, the common things we need to bear in mind when we talk about value are that it is essentially subjective, it involves a trade-off between benefits and sacrifices, that these benefits and sacrifices are made up of many dimensions, and it is always judged relative to alternative competitive offers. Other researchers have offered up useful classifications of types of value which you might also consider. Brock-Smith and Colgate, in their article 'Customer value creation: A practical framework', classify value types as Functional/Instrumental, Experiential, Symbolic and Cost; alternatively Sheth, Newman and Gross in their book *Consumption Values and Market Choices* suggest Functional, Social, Emotional, Epistemic (knowledge) and Conditional value types.

And they say elephants can't dance!

Use the checklist below to capture examples of all of the different types of value you can think of that are relevant to your markets and customers.

1. Economic value—includes price considerations and basic utility of the offer
2. Perceived value—includes brand image and symbolic value
3. Relational value—includes knowledge value
4. Experiential value—includes emotional value

Unlocking the Value Conversation

To improve our understanding of what value means in our company we need a way to capture the different perspectives that might exist. In this way we can bring to the surface differences of understanding and importance.

We define value as:

Value = perceived *relevant and distinct* benefit – total cost of ownership

These exercises will enable you to map out how value is understood in your company. The aim is not to define what customer value definitively means for your customer, but rather the value assumptions and perspectives that occur in your business and ultimately shape the value solutions you create and communicate. These are the value conditions in your markets that your organisation needs to continually and intelligently manage. Economic factors are all about the monetary price the customer pays, such as payment terms or rebates. Perceived factors are the customer's subjective view of value such as product reliability or styling. Relationship factors are about the things that are above and beyond the product, such as expert knowledge and enthusiasm.

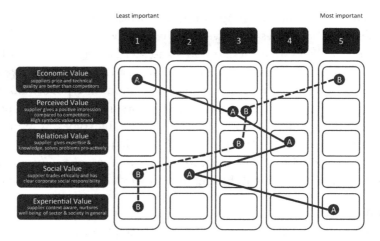

Fig. 1.2 Assessing value types

[Experiential factors are about how working with your company feels overall, such as effortless and ethically good.]

Exercise 1: Customer Value Perspectives

Each member of the team decides what they understand to be the relative importance of each value dimension for the customer. Colour code each person (they can be named, by role or anonymised; we recommend identifying by role). Once this is done join the dots with a coloured line (Fig. 1.2).

Notice similarities and differences. The team should then reflect on these and discuss:

1. Why have these differences occurred?
2. What actions need to be taken on the basis of your discussion?

Exercise 2: Company Value Conversation Bias

This exercise is about where the bias of the value conversation presently lies in your organisation and where it ought to be in future.[1]

In a team or in teams discuss where the focus of attention in the value conversation currently lies. Show this by allocating the fifteen points in the relevant boxes.

---

[1] The bias model is based on an idea originated by Mike Pedlar, John Burgoyne and Tom Boydell in their book *The Learning Company*, where it is used to map management focus on strategy, tactics, management and ideas.

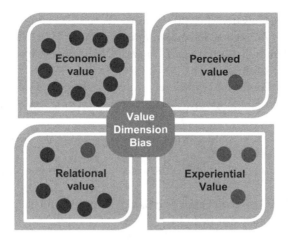

Fig. 1.3 Mapping company value bias

Next think about where the emphasis in the value conversation should go in future. Show this by allocating five points where you believe the emphasis should lie.

Teams should then consider the bias and emphasis shown, compare and contrast perspectives, and discuss the management implications raised by this exercise (Fig. 1.3).

Further Reading on Business to Business Value

Ulaga, W. (2003). Capturing value creation in business relationships: A customer perspective. *Industrial Marketing Management, 32*, 677–693.

Ulaga, W., & Eggert, A. (2005). Relationship value in business markets: The construct and its dimensions. *Journal of Business-to-Business Marketing, 12*(1), 73–99.

References

Ambler, T. (2006). The new dominant logic of marketing. Views of the elephant. In S. L. Vargo & R. F. Lusch (Eds.), *The service dominant logic of marketing. Dialog, debate and directions*. Armonk: M.E.Sharpe.

Anderson, J. C., Jain, D. C., & Chintagunta, P. K. (1993). Customer value assessment in business markets: A state-of-practice study. *Journal of Business to Business Marketing, 1*(1), 3–30.

Argyris, C. (1999). *On organisational learning* (2nd ed.). London: Wiley-Blackwell.

Brock-Smith, J., & Colgate, M. (2007). Customer value creation: A practical framework. *Journal of Marketing Theory and Practice, 15*(1), 7–23, M.E. Sharpe, Inc.

Collins, J., & Porras, J. (2005). *Built to last.* 10th Anniversary edition. London: Random House Business.

Coutelle-Brillet, P., Riviere, A., des Garets, V. (2014). Perceived value of service innovation: A conceptual framework. *Journal of Business & Industrial Marketing, 29*(2), 164–172.

Farmer, D. (1997). Purchasing myopia revisited. *European Journal of Purchasing and Supply Management, 3*, 1–8.

Griffen, A., & Hauser, J.R. (1993). The voice of the customer. *Marketing Science, 12*(1), 1–27

Gronroos, C. (1996). Relationship marketing: Strategic and tactical implications. *Management Decision, 34*(3), 5–14.

Gronroos, C. (2012). Conceptualising value co-creation: A journey to the 1970s and back to the future. *Journal of Marketing Management, 28*(13–14), 1520–1534.

Gummesson, E. (2008). Customer centricity: Reality or wild goose chase. *European Business Review, 20*(4), 315–330.

Holbrook, M. B. (1999). *Consumer value: A framework for analysis and research.* London: Routledge.

Karababa, E., & Kjelgaard, D. (2014). Value in marketing: Towards socio-cultural perspectives. *Marketing Theory, 14*(1), 119–127, Sage.

Khalifa, A. S. (2004). Customer value: A review of recent literature and an integrative configuration. *Management Decision, 42*(5), 645–666.

Leszinski, R., & Marn, M. V. (1997). Setting value, not price. *The McKinsey Quarterly, 1*, 99–115.

Levy, S. J. (1959). Symbols for sale. *Harvard Business Review, 37*, 117–124.

Miles, L. D. (1961). *Techniques of value analysis and engineering.* New York: McGraw-Hill Book Company.

Ng, I. C. L., & Smith, L. (2012). An integrative framework of value. *Review of Marketing Research, Special Issue Toward a Better Understanding of the Role of Value in Market and Marketing, 9*, 207–243.

Porter, M. (1985). *Competitive strategy. Techniques for analysing industries and competitors.* New York: The Free Press.

Porter, M.E., & Kramer, M.R. (2011). Creating Shared Value. *Harvard Business Review.*

Ravald, A., & Gronroos, C. (1996). The value concept and relationship marketing. *European Journal of Marketing, 30*(2), 19–30.

Sheth, J., Newman, B., & Gross, B. (1991). *Consumption values and market choices.* Cincinnati: South-Western.

Tzokas, N., & Saren, M. (1999). Value transformation in relationship marketing. *Australasian Marketing Journal, 7*(1), 52–62.

Ulaga, W. (2003). Capturing value creation in business relationships: A customer perspective. *Industrial Marketing Management, 32*, 677–693.

Vargo, S. L., & Lusch, R. F. (Eds.). (2006). *The service dominant logic of marketing: Dialog, debate, and directions.* Armonk: M.E.Sharpe.

Vargo, S. L., & Lusch, R. F. (2008). Service-dominant logic: Continuing the evolution. *Journal of the Academy of Marketing Science, 36*(1), 1–10, Springer Science & Business Media B.V.

Vargo, S. L., Maglio, P. P., & Akaka, M. A. (2008). On Value and value co-creation: A service systems and service logic perspective. *European Journal of Management, 26*, 145–152.

Westrum, R. (1982). Social intelligence about hidden events: Its significance for scientific research and social policy. *Knowledge: Creation, Diffusion. Utilization, 3*(3), 381–400, Sage Publications Inc.

Westrum, R. (1992). Social intelligence about hidden events. *Knowledge, 3*(3), 381–400.

Woodruff, R. B. (1997). Customer value: The next source for competitive advantage. *Journal of the Academy of Marketing Science, 25*(2), 139–153.

Zeithaml, V. A. (1988). Consumer perceptions of price, quality, and value: A means-end model and synthesis of evidence. *Journal of Marketing, 52*, 2–22.

2

Value Propositions: So What Are They?

In this chapter we will look at:

- What a value proposition is, and is not
- The different levels and types of value propositions
- Why a value proposition approach is important to the growth of your company
- Providing the important first step for effectively implementing a value proposition approach for your customers and your company
- A process for developing value propositions
- Creating a 'golden thread' from market level to individual Customer Value Propositions (CVPs)

So far we have seen that the concept of value is difficult to pin down and contentious. It's a word that means different things to different people. For that reason it's important for your organisation to take time to establish a definition that works for the company and its customers.

The definition of value that we will be moving forward with is the one we outlined in Chap. 1:

Value = perceived relevant and distinct benefit − total cost of ownership

Hopefully you will already have found the tools we gave you to establish 'base camp' in your journey to implement a more effective value-based approach to marketing and selling.

© The Author(s) 2017
S. Kelly et al., *Value-ology*,
DOI 10.1007/978-3-319-45626-3_2

With this in mind, we can turn our attention to a concept that can be equally contentious: value propositions. We thought a story would best illustrate this.

A friend of ours worked for a large tech company in the USA that was acquiring a similar sized company. The chief marketing officer (CMO) position was given to someone from the acquired company who was based on the other side of the country. After a few weeks, the CMO called an 'emergency' value proposition session for a selection of the Vice-Presidents, Directors and Managers in the marketing team, who were told to fly in over the weekend. The purpose of the meeting was not made entirely clear; it seemed to be about deciding what the value proposition of the newly united company was.

Surprise number one was that the CMO did not take part in the whole session, just flitting in and out between other calendar appointments. The task of doing the pre-work for developing the joint company value proposition and presenting it to the broader team had fallen to a couple of managers from the acquired company.

What quickly became apparent was the complete absence of customer value in the work that was being presented. It was all about the combined assets of the company and the 'features' that those assets could provide for customers. Even the people from the acquiring company were talking past each other because they had completely different views of value, depending how close to the customer they were.

A fruitless, frustrating day was spent trying to help refine these capability statements and features. Our friend didn't hang around long in the new company as the difference between this capabilities, feature-led view of value and their overt customer-centred view did not sit well.

Exercise 1: So what do we take from this? Jot down your thoughts about this scenario; now compare them with ours!

The takeaways:

A common definition. Like value it cannot be taken for granted that when you hear the term 'value proposition' that people mean the same thing. We recommend that after you've set on a company view of what value means to you and your customers you should nail down a definition for value propositions so you are talking a common language—not past each other! This becomes a useful tool to use when new hires are brought on board who may come from somewhere where value is viewed in a different way, or not at all. It's clearly very important for mergers and acquisitions to ensure things get off on the right footing. We will look at definitions of value propositions later in the chapter, and will give you tools to help develop value propositions. We will give you the definition we use, so you can carry it through the rest of the book.

Preparation is key. We also think there is a lesson about who should be involved, and what preparation you need to undertake before you call together a session to develop value propositions. Involving customers, in the shape of researching their needs, is something we will discuss more in Chap. 4. We see this as preparation 101. We are also big advocates in heavily involving sales in this process. In business-to-business (B2B) they are the people who are out with the customer, way more often than marketers. How marketing and sales can effectively work together to develop value propositions is the focus of Chap. 9.

It starts at the top. There is also a leadership issue here regarding how involved the CMO should be in this process. We believe that they have to be seen to be taking clear ownership for the value proposition approach and ensuring they involve other stakeholders in the process. Quite how this should be done, and the capabilities required for marketing leadership, are for another book.

What Is a Value Proposition?

We have seen in our example that, like value, the meaning of the term 'value proposition' can be ambiguous and influenced by previous experience. So, after you've got a clear definition of value for your organisation we suggest that the next step is to agree what a value proposition is. By the end of this section you will have our view on this. We have also included some definitions from other authors, as they may help you develop your own definition.

It's About Customer Benefits

The term value proposition is about how value is framed and communicated to the customer prior to purchase. Barnes et al. (2009) describe the evolution of the term value proposition as rooted in the 1950s with the notion of the unique selling proposition (USP). This led to the movement of benefit-led selling, where sales teams were coached to move from product features through to describing customer benefits. Only then did it dawn on organisations that a benefit can only be such if it solves a customer problem, a solution to a need. This is when the term value proposition was conceived.

The origination of the term is credited to McKinsey consultants Bower and Garda (1985), who discussed the making of promises of satisfaction. Lanning and Michaels (1988) built on this, developing consultancy tools that focused on the creation of value propositions. Here a value proposition was defined as a *statement of benefits being offered to a customer group at a price they were willing to pay*. So, a value proposition is traditionally taken to mean the marketing offer of value promise formulated and communicated by the seller, with the intention for it to be accepted by a buyer. If you are embarking on a customer value-led path then you take the view that customers do not buy 'things'; they buy the experiences that the 'things' are able to deliver.

Customer Impact

A value proposition statement is therefore a clear, compelling and credible expression of the experience that a customer will receive from a supplier. Crucially, your value propositions should focus on the projected impact on the customer.

Gronroos and Ravald (2011: 14) provide a useful definition:

> Value propositions are suggestions and projections of what impact on their practices customers can expect. When such a projection is proposed actively to customers, it is a promise about potential future value creation.

A value proposition should communicate the benefits of a product or service in terms that are relevant to the target customer. From the customer's perspective you should illustrate what the actual capability that is offered adds to the customer's business. This can be about adding new revenues, new customers, improving the customer experience or improving operational performance. In short, it should be about moving performance needles that concern the customer.

It's a Promise for the Future

We can see that this involves giving customers an understanding of how the future can be better than the present. They may be able to improve efficiency or agility, or benefit from profitable new revenues.

Monetary Calculation

In B2B it's generally accepted, though less widely practised, that this should involve some monetary calculation of the benefits that will be delivered that are seen to outweigh costs. We will provide you with examples and templates later in the chapter.

It's Unique

A former Sales Vice-President colleague used to like pointing out that if you compared value proposition statements from different companies they all looked the same. He used to revel in presenting a selection of value propositions to colleagues with the company names removed, and challenging them to find their own company value propositions. Why don't you try it? What does this tell you?

Exercise 2: Could you find your own value propositions? Just a quick scan of a few of your competitors' websites probably shows that everyone says things like: we are innovative, we are the best in class, we provide excellent customer service.

You should strive for unique value propositions that set you apart. Remember that just because it's unique doesn't mean it's useful. You should be aiming to demonstrate how you can uniquely deliver customer value in terms that the customer recognises as value.

It's Based on Deep Customer Understanding

So here's the rub. You should have already figured out that value propositions are promises of value you hope to deliver to the customer in the future. This cannot be done unless you are clear about what is valuable to the customer. A level of effort is required in order to understand customers and their issues.

This is something that we will help you with in Chap. 4. The upsides are certainly there to be seen. Aberdeen Group showed that companies who leveraged online resources to improve customer understanding typically improved revenues by 21 %.

Drawing all this together we can say that our definition of a value proposition is:

A value proposition is a promise of expected future value, illustrating that future relevant and distinct benefits will outweigh the total cost of ownership

A value proposition should include:

- Impact—how it will positively impact the customer organisation
- Capability—what it is that you can do for the customer to make this impact
- Spend (Costs)—how much the customer will be expected to pay for the privilege
- Monetary calculation—of the financial benefits minus costs
- Unique—things that set you apart from competitors
- Alignment—to the key needs of the customer

Additionally it may include:

- An emotional dimension, for example relating to the peace of mind the customer can expect
- A relational dimension, if the customer and your organisation are looking for benefits that will accrue from an enhanced relationship

So, to hit all the right notes and resonate with your customer a value proposition should be MUSICAL:

- Monetary calculation—of financial benefits minus costs
- Unique—things that set you apart from competitors
- Spend (costs)—how much the customer is prepared to pay
- Impact—how it will positively impact the customer organisation
- Capability—what it is that you can do for the customer to make this impact
- ALigned—to the key needs of the customer

Using this framework we recommend that before you start developing value propositions you agreed on a clear definition on what it is for your organisation.

Ultimately, for a value proposition to be most compelling and relevant it needs to be aimed at an individual in a B2B customer organisation who has some influence on the buying decision. We recognise that there will have been a lot of exposure to other communications from your company that need to reflect this value-based approach. We shall see later that the perception potential customers form about you can influence whether they even let your sales rep through the door!

Before we deal with that, let's explore why value propositions are important and relevant.

Why Are Value Propositions Important?

It may be recognised that for any organisation providing customers with something they value that is different and better than competitors is increasingly a challenge. In a world where technology moves quickly, having a product advantage over a long period of time is a pipe-dream.

It's Not All About the Product

Even if sustained product differentiation was possible, is it really what customers want? When Forrester asked Fortune 500 C suite executives involved in buying decisions why they chose a certain vendor, only 16 % cited a vendor's products, services or capabilities to be the most important factor separating them from the pack. Executives overwhelmingly believed that vendors who understood their business problems and could prescribe solutions to them were the ones who won out. Despite this only 27 % of C-level executives found salespeople knowledgeable about their business.

In *Agile Selling* Jill Konrath notes that buyers increasingly keep sellers out because in their experience most are 'Product-pushing peddlers who don't bring any value to the decision making process, ask stupid questions, offer minimal insights and give boring presentations'. A C-level respondent to the Forrester survey echoed this! 'I just spent the last 30 minutes with a salesperson in a well-known company who gave me a stack of brochures almost as big as a phone book to look through. It's as if he expected me to wade through all of that material to find the needles in the haystack for how they can help me.'

Relevant Customer Insight

The good news is that studies by the Corporate Executive Board (CEB) seem to show that it's in the hands of sales. Their research showed that the biggest differentiator during a sale was the sales experience itself. 53 % of customers said their loyalty was enhanced by the sales rep—if they bring valuable help and insights, versus 19 % who quoted product and service delivery and 19 % who mentioned brand and company impact. So if you bring insight into the sales process and show understanding of the customer's business you're providing the differentiation in the approach.

Of course, this is not the whole story any more. CEB research also showed that B2B buyers tend to be over 60 % of the way through the buying process before they contact a sales person. In *Frugalnomics*, Pisello (2015), points out that 67 % of B2B buyers say they have a clear picture of what they want when they first contact a sales rep.

This suggests that having a value-based conversation with the customer begins with marketing. While salespeople will always strive to be involved in the buying process earlier marketing will often have to take care of the front 60 %, if we take on board the CEB research. At the same time, 94 % of potential customers have disengaged with vendors because they received irrelevant content (CEB). So your marketing team needs to get a lot better at creating relevant content that customers value with a value proposition that resonates with the issues they face. Otherwise they will have checked out of your electronic building before they call your sales team.

There is ample evidence to demonstrate that the sunny uplands are worth striving for. Ninety-one percent of executives said they would happily forward marketing content if they found it insightful and relevant (Corporate Executive Board).

The Value Proposition Approach Could Be the Difference

Declaring our hand, if it wasn't already obvious, we agree with Malcolm McDonald, Emeritus Professor of Marketing at Cranfield, a top UK business school. Like him, we hold the view that in a world where product differentiation is difficult the value proposition approach can be the factor that makes the difference in the market, giving you an advantage over your competitors. His research has shown that only 5 % of organisations are using financially quantifiable value propositions; so there is clearly an opportunity for you to set yourself apart.

Value Propositions Deliver Results

McDonald and Oliver (2016) believe that financially justified value propositions help you increase profitable sales in a number of ways:

- You will close typically between 2 % and 10 % more deals
- You will reduce discounting by 20–30 %
- You can develop more productive marketing campaigns, demonstrating value
- You will reduce the number of no or delayed decisions

We can certainly concur with these numbers. We witnessed an increase in win rate of 6 % when we worked with a US organisation to ensure all their bid responses included numeric value propositions. We helped a large UK corporation gain record revenue growth for three consecutive years through adoption of an 'all-in' value proposition-based approach. You could do this too, by following the approach laid out in this book.

If There's No Value All You're Left With is Price

Finally, if you haven't developed deep customer understanding, if you've not been able to make sense of how your company can help customers solve business problems, then you have not unlocked the door to creating customer value. You will recognise if that's where you are as the conversation will rush straight to price. Unless you can be sure that you're the lowest cost competitor this is the road to hell. Research typically shows that a 5 % reduction in price results in a 16 % drop in profitability.

So, what's it to be, a 10 % uplift in closed deals or a 16 % drop in profitability? Do you want to provide customers with insight and understanding about their key issues and how to fix them, or just get beaten up on price? We can help you take the path to the sunny uplands, away from the road to hell.

> In an increasingly competitive world, where products are often the same, the value proposition approach can be the factor that sets you apart in the market

Our Approach: The Value Proposition System

So what you are ultimately striving for is value propositions that resonate with individual customers inside the companies that you hope to sell to. For this approach to be effective we believe, like Webster (2002), that value propositions should be the 'single most important organizing principle' for companies.

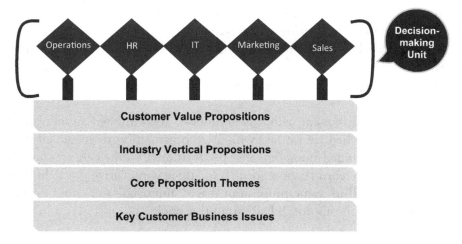

Fig. 2.1 Value proposition stack

What do we mean by that? Simply that value should resound through all levels of dialogue between your organisation and its customers, and drive the creation and development of offers and solutions. The approach needs to be coherent and consistent on the company website aimed at all business customers, in communications to different customer segments or industry sectors through a customer organisation, and even down to an individual customer within that organisation. We call this approach the 'value proposition stack'.

The rest of this chapter will give you a brief overview of this process and introduce some tools and templates. From Chap. 3 onwards we will flesh out this approach in more detail, show how it links to developing solutions, messaging and campaigns, and how it helps with value proposition conversations with the customers (Fig. 2.1).

Understanding Key Business Issues

At the bottom of the stack are customer business issues, creating the foundation layer for building value propositions. We will cover the type of research you can perform to get an understanding of key customer business issues in Chap. 4.

If 100 B2B marketing and salespeople wrote a list of the typical issues customers face they would probably not be wildly different, so why not try it:

Exercise 3: Write a list of issues that you think your business customers face

So what's on your list? Some of the things we covered in the value proposition definition section are probably there: revenue, costs, profits, customer growth and acquisition, customer satisfaction, competitive advantage, regulatory concerns, productivity and operational performance factors. These kind of factors, or key customers drivers as Jeff Thull calls them in *The Prime Solution*, affect all business organisations in different ways. While public sector organisations may not be concerned about financial profit they will certainly be concerned about service provision to citizens and will want to see a fair return on their investment.

We recognise that these factors change in terms of importance at the macro level, within the markets the customers operate and in relation to the competitive performance of the individual organisation. At the time of writing the price of Brent crude oil is around $28 a barrel; it was over $100 a barrel less than a year ago. This affects the fortunes of a lot of companies in many ways. Getting to a point of understanding of the key issues affecting your customer base at a point in time, and having a system for refreshing this, is the aim of this step. When these are taken together with the concerns that come out of the World Economic Forum each year, it's probably high time for you to refresh your view of the key issues that are affecting your customers right now. Having learning agility here can provide you with better insight into your customers than your competitors. This gives you a platform to develop customer proposition themes, which is the next step in our approach.

Developing Proposition Themes

What we are advocating here is that what comes out of the evaluation of customer business issues should shape the key proposition themes that you use to develop your approach. We will show how to get to these themes in more depth in Chap. 5. How many you go with is up to you, but for reasons that will become obvious when we get to the campaign and messaging chapters we think it should be no more than three, or four at a stretch. We advocate that you should tie your solutions, offers, products, messaging and campaigns to these proposition themes.

The benefits of this approach are:

• You demonstrate to the customer through all your communications that you are trying to make a difference or 'add value' to their business

- It provides a discipline to use customer issues as a starting point for all your conversations
- You will not be bombarding them with irrelevant, disjointed messages that jump from product to product
- You will save marketing money as you can array all your products and solutions under these themes
- You will make more money, as in our experience if you use this approach you don't have a cross-sell, up-sell problem; therefore you're not selling one product at a time

The themes that you select should:

- Capture the essence of the key customer issues that you feel your company can address
- Resonate with customers as something they are aspiring to achieve
- Be broad and flexible enough to allow sector, segment and customer tailoring as you move up the value stack towards financially justified individual CVPs

Some common pitfalls you need to avoid are:

- Don't be too generic in the way you communicate these themes; this is a common complaint that salespeople have. The President of Sales of a US-based global ICT (information and communications technology) company recently told us: 'Some of the marketing communication is so generic it's just not helpful either to the customer or to the sales folks.' Make sure you provide insight about the issues that led you to the themes.
- Don't make the top level themes too restrictive. A Segment Marketing Director of a global IT (information technology) supplier said: 'We have a small number of themes which we are supposed to use to guide our communication. Unfortunately a couple of them don't really apply to my customer set.'
- Make sure your value themes or your corporate value proposition are about customers or you've blown it straight away. We know a US organisation that says it provides 'industry leading technology'. Well, one of its divisions can't really say that, but who cares; it's got nothing to do with customer value anyway.

More on how to get to the themes in Chaps. 4 and 5.

Industry Vertical Propositions or Segment Propositions

OK, so super-purist text book marketers may say that the starting point of this kind of approach should be developing customer 'segments', where a segment is a group of customers that you have identified have similar needs. We would largely agree with this, which is why we cover buyer personas in later chapters. Here we are trying to help you address your current reality. We know from our own experience that you need to communicate to all your business customers, so up until now we've given you an approach that gives you value themes that are grounded on customer issues. We recognise that the closer you get to the customer the more resonant your value propositions become. We just don't want you to blow it with product blah blah and by talking irrelevant nonsense about yourself further upstream.

We also recognise that many industries organise their sales teams into industry sectors. So the next step is to take the proposition themes and ask yourself how they play out in the customer sectors you serve. For example, if your theme is 'productivity', what are the key productivity challenges in retail financial services? What are the key productivity KPIs (key performance indicators) used? What insight can you provide about how to impact productivity in this sector? There may also be sector-specific issues you identify that you can place under the theme.

Customer Value Propositions (CVPs)

Of course not all the customers in your sales sectors are the same. If you look at the performance of UK food retailers over the last two or three years you will know that some have been affected more than others by the incursion of Aldi and Lidl at the low-price end of the market. All have been affected, in some way, by changes in buying behaviour away from one big weekly shop to less more often habits.

It's good to be reminded that each customer is different. We saw a C-level financial services customer say to the sales audience of a large vendor: 'Don't treat me like any other financial services company: recognise that I have unique issues and challenges.' The expectation is that you understand the financial services industry and its challenges along with the unique position and challenges of each company.

If you embrace this approach then you should be performing a deep level of research into your customers. Through this you can identify their unique challenges and develop company level value proposition statements that signal your understanding of how you can help them solve some of the problems they are facing. Given the work that has gone before there should be good alignment between the customers issues, the sector issues and the overall value themes you selected earlier in the process.

Going through this exercise will also help you form a view about which of your products and services can help the customer solve each of their problems. You will need to develop value propositions for each of these solutions which demonstrate that you understand what performance needles you are moving for the customer, and how you can do it better than your competitors. Below we give an example of this type of value proposition, inspired by a real value proposition adapted from a previous company engagement, and which led to a sale:

Example Call Centre Value Proposition

Money Bank PLC will be able to improve *customer retention by 10 % or $500,000 annually* through the ability to handle all incoming calls as a result of implementing an *integrated call centre for $300,000.*

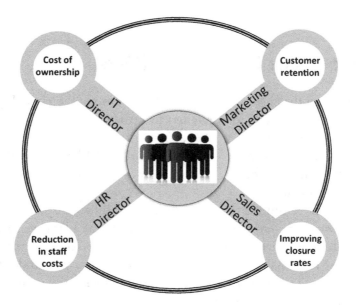

Fig. 2.2 Value Propositions differ by C Level Officer

By September 2017, the company will be able to demonstrate the delivery of value *by improved customer retention and revenue growth.*

We have included some templates at the end of this chapter to help with this approach.

Exercise 4: So how MUSICAL is the value proposition in Fig. 2.2? How could you improve it? Write down your thoughts and compare them with ours.

M—yes, it has clear monetary calculation of promised value

U—there is nothing about what is unique in the offer, though the approach itself was unique

S—yes, there is a clear line of sight of the cost of the call centre

I—yes, it gives a monetary view of the impact

C—apart from mentioning the call centre, it doesn't say much about the capability

AL—yes, this is ALigned with need for the customer to increase customer retention

So, all in all it is a good value proposition which needs to say more about uniqueness and capability to make it resonate and be fully MUSICAL!

You are probably thinking that this part of the process looks like account planning with a twist, or account-based marketing (ABM), as it's now being called. We agree that it is, and we'll be covering ABM in more detail in Chap. 8. You may also be thinking, especially if you're in sales, that it could be possible to skip the earlier parts of the process and just start from here; after all, that's what you've always done. At one level we would agree it is possible to start here, but there are a number of big pitfalls.

The first one we will illustrate by example:

In a recent conversation a Marketing Director for a large global IT organisation led us to believe that he had the whole value proposition approach nailed down as he had embarked on an intense programme of ABM. The major contradiction was that he did not have any clear idea of how his company differentiated itself from competitors as the industry was 'commoditised'. So while he was going through this ABM exercise it was apparent that competitive advantage, or lack of it, was still being viewed through a product lens. A lens, which research has shown, customers are less and less interested in.

Had this ABM activity been taking place inside our 'all-in' value-based approach the customer themes would have provided the lens through which to articulate customer value. This in itself should provide you with a value advantage, because research tells us that most of your competitors will be ploughing the product furrow. It will also help you think about competitive advantage from the standpoint of how you can make your customers more 'agile' or 'productive' in a way your competitors can't.

The major drawback of starting from here is that each day you have a value conversation with your 'account', your company marketing is likely to be product focused and your customer is likely to be overwhelmed by product feature-speak. This can only serve to dilute your ABM efforts.

Individual Customer Value Propositions (CVPs)

True relevance and resonance is achieved when you get to the top layer of the value stack. Recent CEB research showed that on average there are 5.4 people involved in making a major purchase decision in a B2B buying process. The signs are that decision-making became more consensus-based during the last recession and has stayed that way. Many sales methodologies encourage us to 'segment' people inside customer organisations as decision-makers, end users and technical buyers. Some encourage you to get a 'coach' inside the customer to help you navigate inside the customer organisation. Through experience we know that many organisations focus too much on the technical buyer. This is the person who probably wrote the invitation to tender, who may not have a full understanding of the value the organisation is looking to get from the purchase.

Our approach acknowledges that there will be on average 5.4 people involved in any B2B purchase who may all be looking for different types of value. This involves thinking through the value that each person is looking for.

In the simple example above we can see that each of the C level officers will get different value from a purchase of call centre technology. The chief information officer will probably be looking for something that integrates well with current technology and is easy to maintain, in other words something that has a low cost of ownership. The President of Sales will respond to a value proposition that shows how the call centre will help increase sales closure rates. Here you can present a revenue stream that delivers a return to help move the dialogue away from costs. The CMO may be compelled by a customer retention proposition or by generating new leads, depending on the context. The head of HR (Human Resources) may be interested in knowing how people retention could be improved through creation of a better call centre environment. This looks simple, but getting to the point that you can craft these individual value propositions is not easy. It demands that you have conversations with these individuals to understand their personal challenges. Of course, if you've done this before you can provide insights into how much you have improved performance. In our view there is no substitute for the value conversations with the 5.4 individuals you need to influence. The next chapter is devoted specifically to value conversations based on some unique research performed by Dr. Paul Johnston into how value is created in sales conversations.

Don't Forget the Follow Up

Hopefully by now it's clear that value propositions are promises of future value. Crafting compelling value propositions that resonate with individuals supported by our 'all-in' value-based approach should mean that all marketing and sales interactions begin and end with customer value in-mind. We have seen how this approach can lead to enhanced revenue and profit.

It is important to remember that value propositions are *promises* of future value. Thull pointed out that many organisations are on their third iteration of customer relationship management systems because promised value was not delivered. Crucially they were too difficult and time-consuming for the end-users who had to input the customer data.

In their work on service dominant-logic, Vargo and Lusch remind us that value can only be realised during consumption, or in use. Here is where most organisations seem to miss a pretty significant trick. The question is, even if you are following a value proposition approach, do you ever follow up with the customer to see if the benefits or value promises you made are being delivered? In our experience most companies would have to say no, if they were being completely honest. What is the worst that can happen if you start to do this as a matter of routine? Inevitably, in a B2B context, the customer is probably on the hook to do something to help ensure the promised value was realised. In our view, building in follow-up conversations about value delivered can expose new problems that you can help with, keep you in control of the conversation and in touch with key players in the customer organisation. Crucially it will give you exposure to end users, who become more of a focus once your solution is being used by your customer.

Hopefully you will now have had the conversations in your organisation to allow you to advance from base camp. It should now be clear what value and value propositions mean for you and your organisation. If you want to follow our process you can see that the next step is to gain a clear understanding of the issues facing your customers; more of this in Chap. 4. This will serve as a bedrock on which you can build your value approach; which will help you develop value themes. This starts to drive a cohesive approach to all your customer interactions, and the customer will soon see that the conversations are now more about them and less about you. Ultimately the aim is to develop resonating individual value propositions, and this is where we turn next: value conversations.

Further Reading

Anderson, J. C., Narus, J.A., & Van Rossum, W.. (2006, March). Customer value propositions in business markets. *Harvard Business Review 84*(3), 91–99.

Barnes, C., Blake, H., & Pinder, D. (2009). *Creating and delivering your value proposition: Managing customer experience for profit.* Kogan Page.

Bower, M., & Garda, R. A. (1985). The role of marketing in management. *The McKinsey Quarterly, 3,* 34–46.

Gronroos, C., & Ravald, A. (2011). Service as business logic: Implications for value creation and marketing. *Journal of Service Management., 22*(1), 5–22.

Lanning, M., & Michaels, E. (1988, July). A business is a value delivery system. McKinsey Staff Paper No. 41.

Pisello, T. (2015a). *Frugalnomics survival guide: How to use your unique value to market better, stand out and sell more.* Winter Park: Alinean Press.

Webster, F. E. (2002a). *Market-driven management: How to define, develop, and deliver customer value* (2nd ed.). Hoboken: Wiley.

3

The Value Proposing Professional

In this chapter we will look at:

- Understanding your personal value
- Understanding pre-emptive value judgements
- Understanding the value of reading customer context
- Understanding meaningful value dialogue
- Understanding the value of being relevant
- The arts of the value-proposing professional

You Create Value Too

This isn't just some self-help affirmation to make you feel good about yourself. Our in depth qualitative research study of fifty senior key sales and marketing professionals shows that your social abilities are central to the application of value-ology and the process of unlocking and creating customer value. Studies have shown that we make value judgements about other people in a matter of seconds. This means that we can't always rely on customers to make an entirely objective assessment of our value proposition.

Most of us tend to take our social skills for granted. Human beings are social animals and we hone our social skills from an early age. Things such as our ability to make people feel at ease in our presence, our ability to respect others, our ability to anticipate how people feel and even how we know what to say and what not to say in certain situations.

© The Author(s) 2017
S. Kelly et al., *Value-ology*,
DOI 10.1007/978-3-319-45626-3_3

All of these things create an impression on other people, and we devote much of our social lives to presenting an impression of ourselves that we hope other people will value and respect. Creating the right impression is an essential social competence that lies at the heart of value-ology. Back in 1977 Lynn Shostack, philanthropist, writer and former vice-president of Citibank, emphasised in her article 'Breaking free from product marketing' the crucial role people play in creating value, when she observed that 'services are often inextricably entwined with their human representatives. In many fields, a person is perceived to be the service.'

Social competence adds real value to the skills of sales management, decision-making and sales psychology we might already possess. In the majority of sales and marketing text books the social competence of sales professionals is glossed over or simply missing. Of course reference is often made to the need for the sales professional to establish rapport, be a good listener, show empathy and be emotionally intelligent.[1] More specialised popular psychology books describe the way our minds work and explain techniques for coping with anxiety, anger and rejection,[2] understanding the mindsets of others,[3] and how to communicate, influence and persuade.[4] However, there is a huge gap in explaining what goes on when sales professionals go through the act of proposing value to their customers. This is the world of supplier–customer social interactions. How salespeople actually perform in the presence of others belongs to what we call *the missing middle* of our understanding of sales and marketing management. It is the world of the *value-proposing professional*.

- Sales process management and customer decision-making
  - The missing middle—supplier-customer social interactions
- Psychological techniques of selling

In the following sections we will explain exactly what is going on in the missing middle and what sales professionals need to do to become true value-proposing professionals.

---

[1] Emotional intelligence is the idea of Daniel Goleman, who identified a range of socio-psychological attributes of people who were good at relating to others.

[2] *The Chimp Paradox* by Steve Peters is an excellent book that explains how our brains work for and against us in high performance situations.

[3] *Mindset* by Carol S. Dweck explains how each of us frames the world differently in our minds.

[4] These include techniques such as neuro-linguistic programming and Bob Cialdini's principles of social influence and persuasion.

Your Personal Value

It's true that we sort of 'know' when we are in the presence of a capable professional. We recognise in an instant if someone is talking bull and baloney or if they are worth spending time listening to. When we meet a good salesperson we often talk of their personal charm, charisma and persuasiveness. It's common for people to say (usually as a backhanded compliment) that good salespeople have a mysterious ability to charm the birds off the trees, sell snow to an Inuit or even sell sawdust to a sawmill.

Many sales training companies handshake this view of the ubiquitous qualities of the salesperson by quoting famed author Robert Louis Stevenson, who in one of his less well-known books written in 1982, titled *Across the Plains with other Memories and Essays*, observed that 'everyone lives by selling something'. Stevenson noticed that in any form of social interaction people try to convince others of their personal worth as well as the value of the goods and services they supply. The view that selling is an essential aspect of all human activity is also emphasised in Daniel Pink's 2014 bestseller *To Sell Is Human*, where on page 19 he observes:

> Physicians sell patients on remedy. Lawyers sell juries on a verdict. Teachers sell students on the value of paying attention in class. Entrepreneurs woo funders, writers sweet talk producers, coaches cajole players.

Many of us find it difficult to say exactly what it is that effective sales professionals do well. These things are intangible and difficult to measure. There has, of course, been a lot of formal academic research into trying to find the answer. This research tends to fall into two main types: research that examines sales management and the buying process or research into the traits and techniques of the effective sales professional.

Types of Professional Sales Research

Research into Sales Process Management Customer Decision-making

These studies analyse and objectively describe each step of supplier–customer interaction with the aim of structuring the decisions sales executives need to make along the way. By analysing buyer decision-making, models are created that show how the process starts with a realisation of a need, then the search and selection of alternatives through to purchase negotiation and decision-making. Studies of buying process and customer engagement include *managing the sales funnel*, which is the process of classifying customer types and reducing a large number of potential customers to a small number of actual customers (see Miller et al. 2005, 2012), *managing the relationship ladder*, which models how transactional buyers are progressively converted into relationally minded customers and ultimately partners (see Payne et al. 1998) and *consultative selling behaviours* (see Rackham 1995), following the Huthwaite proprietary SPIN method that moves a customer from a vague awareness and articulation of their problems and needs to acceptance and purchase of a proposed solution.

More recently, the work of Matthew Dixon and Brent Adamson has promoted the idea of *The Challenger Sale*,[5] which is set out in their 2011 book of the same name—which is how to take control of the customer conversation. The authors claim that the era of relationship selling is passé and superseded by an era where sales professionals unsettle and critique the world view of the customer and educate him/her with new and provocative insights about the market.

Research into Psychological Techniques of Selling

These studies make use of insights from cognitive and social psychology regarding how we process and make sense of information, how we communicate, how to change attitudes, what motivates us, and even how our neurology affects our thinking and behaviour. Studies that look at salesperson traits and techniques approach things from a psychological perspective to help sales executives, classify types of buyer, get past gatekeepers, overcome objections, uncover problems through re-framing and probing questions, influence and persuade customers using particular language structures and words, and negotiating techniques. (see Jobber and Lancaster 2014; Pink 2012; Hogan 1996; Cialdini 2000).

A review of these different types of research into business-to-business (B2B) selling shows that there are far fewer studies carried out on the social dimensions of supplier–customer interaction. It's as if the middle ground of sales

---

[5] For an interesting critique of the research methodology and findings used by Dixon and Adamson see Adam Rapp, Daniel G. Bachrach, Nikolaos Panagopoulos and Jessica Ogilvie (2014) 'Salespeople as knowledge brokers: A review and critique of the challenger sales model', *Journal of Personal Selling & Sales Management*, 34:4, 245–259.

understanding has been overlooked or simply taken for granted because we just assume salespeople are 'good with people'.

We believe there is even more to be learned about the way value is created from the social perspective. Our research clears up some of the mystery surrounding professional value mentioned above and what is really going on when an effective salesperson is 'good with people'. It is nevertheless important to realise that this perspective *adds to* our understanding of sales interactions rather than replacing the other perspectives. They all play a part in effective value creation. Our research has identified some clear and practical capabilities that contribute to how B2B sales professionals unlock value by giving the impression of professional competence and likability.

True value-proposing professionals are liked not simply because they are charismatic, similar in attitude and outlook to yourself, or great to be around. They also have a way of showing a deep and informed understanding of the customer's world, the problems and issues he/she faces and an ability to come up with creative ways to move the customer's business forward. They are respectful and humble, and at the same time can assert ideas and options. They are commercially astute and have a mature outlook, and crucially they have the capability to unlock customer value. We would certainly agree with Matthew Dixon and Brent Adamson that being a critical friend who challenges the customer is more valuable than just being an all-round 'nice guy'.

Supplier–Customer Social Interactions: What Does the Missing Middle Look Like?

The missing middle is a zone of inter-personal value creation. Our research shows that this is the zone where the sales professional demonstrates:

• Ability to read and tune into the social norms, expectations and values of different and diverse customer settings and behave accordingly.
• Ability to produce insightful and relevant interpretations about the problems and issues facing the customer.
• Ability to 'park' personal views of value by showing respect to what the customer deems to be most relevant.
• Ability to 'suppose' and invite dialogue on 'what if' rather than exclusively focus on 'selling' just what's in the catalogue
• Ability to be adaptable and open minded.

Customer value is unlocked by B2B sales professionals who are highly competent in social interactions and have an informed capability to read and deeply understand what's going in the world of the customer. They do more than manage processes and deploy tactical sales techniques. They operate strategically on a human and social level.

Richard Bagozzi of the University of Michigan, in his 2006 article titled 'The role of social and self-conscious emotions in the regulation of business to business relationships in salesperson–customer interactions', brings home this point when he says:

> Business relationships do not endure and flourish on their own ... buyers and sellers do more than follow well defined scripts in accordance with codified rules ... if this were all there was firms could computerise much of business to business transactions ... and do away with most of the human element.

Enduring, creative and open business relationships are only possible through face-to-face communication.[6]

It is clear therefore that sales professionals play an absolutely pivotal role in the creation of customer value at the social level during face to face interactions. We believe that it is a mistake to treat B2B salespeople as just another choice in the communications mix alongside advertising, sales promotion, direct mail and public relations. Doing this risks your sales team acting as if they are simply 'talking brochures' or being dismissed as inexperienced 'space cadets', as one of the people we interviewed described them. In a B2B context, effective sales professionals act as experienced consultants and facilitators with the ability to help customers think differently about the problems and issues they face and the types of solution that might be appropriate. They are in that sense a trusted critical friend.

Understanding Sales Professionals as Value-Proposing Actors

The term *actor* is used by academic researchers to refer to any organisation, department, group or person that takes action in the real world. The idea of the value-proposing actor brings together the two central concepts we have covered in previous chapters, namely value and value proposition.

---

[6] Sheena Leek and Peter Turnbull's IMP conference paper 'Interpersonal contacts in business markets: The impact of information technology' provides an interesting discussion of the significance of face-to-face communication for business marketing.

The important point we want to make here is that the inter-personal act of *proposing* value matters as much as the value *proposition* itself. When we propose something to a customer we are co-creating value as we do it.

The term value-proposing actor originates in a list of premises that outline Stephen Vargo and Robert Lusch's service dominant logic theory. Premise seven states:

> The enterprise cannot deliver value, but only offer value propositions. (Vargo and Lusch 2011)

Therefore the people who work for the enterprise as sales professionals similarly can only offer value propositions. What Vargo and Lusch are driving at here is that customer value is not added into the product and service prior to purchase and use. Customer value is created as the product or service is being used and it can only ever be determined by the customer. Logically this means that the potential customer value of any offer or solution can only be *proposed* rather than *pre-given* by the supplier: hence the label value-*proposing* actor.

For example, there is the case of internationally renowned wholesale paper and board company Stora Enso from Scandinavia. They operate in what seems to be a highly commoditised market. Many of their competitors offer a substantial volume discount on a cardboard used in fast food packaging, which they offer as an alternative to the premium board typically sold by Stora Enso. The potential of huge direct cost savings over long production runs might seem like a good deal on the face of it. However, the technical specification of the alternative board compromises on some highly specialised aspects of the product. Using it creates production problems, which cause downtime, waste and missed deliveries because it doesn't feed properly through the printing machines. The real value of the proposed value offer to the customer is obviously much less attractive than promised. Whilst appealing economic value was proposed by the competitors, the value in use experienced by the customer (in this case a mix of economic, relational and experiential value) was commercially catastrophic.

Although Vargo and Lusch originally used the idea of the value-proposing actor to refer to organization-to-organisation interactions, more recently several researchers have used the term to specifically refer to customer-facing staff such as sales professionals and key account managers. Jasmin Baumann and Kenneth Le Meunier-FitzHugh of Norwich Business School and Paul Johnston and Simon Kelly of Sheffield Business School (both in the UK) have looked closely at sales professionals as value-proposing actors and how they co-create value during the evolution of customer relationships. In this research, the crucial role of communication, collaboration and knowledge exchange is emphasised. This research is informed by the work of David Ballantyne and Richard Varey (2006), in their article 'Creating value-in-use through marketing interaction', who suggest that value proposition creation is essentially an act of interactive communication. In this sense Baumann and Le Meunier-FitzHugh explain how the salesperson acts as a *translator* of the customer voice back to the organisation.

What this means is that the salesperson has considerable strategic significance in ensuring the firm's value proposition becomes a reality. In a B2B context Professor Chris Blocker of the University of Tennessee, Joseph Cannon, Nikolaos G. Panagopoulos and Jeffrey K. Sager explain the significance of this in their 2012 article 'The role of the sales force in value creation and appropriation: New directions for research' when they say:

> Salespeople operate at the boundaries of their firms with buyers and are in the best position to not only adapt to initial and ongoing changes in customer needs but also to anticipate customers' future desires.

Impression Management

The fundamental role of face-to-face communication in the co-creation of value is not simply restricted to verbal exchanges. In 1959 US sociologist Erving Goffman in his book *The Presentation of Self in Everyday Life* (1990) introduced the metaphor of drama to explain how the manner of someone's performance during an interaction creates a particular impression in the minds of the other people. The salesperson in this context is regarded as an actor on a stage (note that this is a different use of the term actor to that mentioned in service dominant logic above).

Many of us will be familiar with how the idea of impression has been used as the basis for creating a personal brand and using body language. These techniques are often used to create an initial personal image through dress sense and style and to establish rapport by getting rid of habits such as folding your arms when speaking, which creates a subconscious barrier between you and the person you are speaking with. Whilst these things matter, of course, they don't really address the whole idea of performance and what is really meant by presenting an appropriate impression.

We are all in the business of creating a social impression, from showing we are busy and engaged, to signalling we are laid back and relaxed, from appearing sporty and athletic to looking cultured and intellectual. When we do this Goffman calls our behaviour *dramatic realisation*. This is how the salesperson demonstrates the invisible (hard to put your finger on things mentioned above) aspects of his/her capability, such as social awareness, respect for others, diligence and so on.

The reason we engage in dramatic realisation is because in most everyday situations we want to be taken seriously by other people. Erving Goffman says our need to be taken seriously lies at the heart of all social interactions. Our research confirms that experienced sales professionals work very hard at being taken seriously. You can see, therefore, that being taken seriously by the customer is quite separate from the attributes of the particular goods or services being offered for sale.

For the B2B sales professionals to be taken seriously they must establish the impression that they are trustworthy, helpful, dependable and knowledgeable. This leads to establishing eligibility and credibility as a supplier. A key account manager of a university business engagement team summed this up during our research:

> We need to come across as a safe pair of hands and what that means is track record, experience, intellectual credentials, gravitas as a people.

You may wish to pause and reflect here. Does your organisation make conscious decisions about the impression you want your salespeople to leave the customer with? Do you want to be seen as a 'safe pair of hands', collaborative, insightful, innovative... What is your customer looking for in the people they buy from?

Becoming a Value-Proposing Professional

With the idea of the value-proposing actor in mind we can now start to talk of the sales professional as a value-proposing professional. As we have mentioned, there is extensive research that identifies desirable and valued attributes of effective salespeople and key account managers from the buyer's perspective.[7] These range from regularity of contact and following up, product and market knowledge, helpfulness, concern and support of the customer's business, tact and politeness, conscientiousness, involving others and adaptiveness.

These attributes identify and describe what is typically expected by the buyer from the seller over the course of a business relationship. As well as

---

[7] See Alvin Williams and John Seminerio (1985) – What Buyers Like From Salesmen in Industrial Marketing Management (14) and Paolo Guenzi, Catherine Pardo, Laurent Georges (2007) Relational selling strategy and key account managers' relational behaviors: An exploratory study in Industrial Marketing Management (36).

knowing what these particular attributes are, our research shows how effective salespeople can unlock value by doing three very specific things:

- Anticipating customer value
- Understanding the social dimensions of buying situations
- Understanding what is relevant to the customer

We will now look at each of these in turn.

Being Able to Anticipate Customer Value

Good sales professionals are skilled at knowing in advance what value looks like in their market sector, and balancing the different facets of value that matter to different stakeholders. This insight challenges the assumption found in most sales and marketing text books that the best approach to business planning and management is to 'do objective research' before anything else. Of course this approach seems very sensible and logical, a sort of management 'look before you leap'. It follows the linear/rational step-by-step decision making approach found in many management publications. The classic format recommends doing a situation audit and analysis, establishing aims and objectives, devising strategies and tactics, and measuring effectiveness.

This is often stated as establishing:

- Where are we?
- Where do we want to be?
- How are we going to get there?
- How will we know if we have arrived?

In competitive marketing strategy, this is the use of decision-making and analysis tools such as PEST analysis, Five Forces analysis, Ansoff's Matrix, SWOT analysis, market segmentation, targeting, positioning and marketing mix,[8] and the general format is applied at the tactical level of sales and account management too.

If we take a relational view of value, though, we know that B2B exchanges occur not just as single transactions, but are combined into what Christian Gronroos (2000) in his book *Service Management and Marketing* calls episodes and sequences. This means that unless a B2B executive is entering an

---

[8] See Glossary for explanations.

entirely unknown market or engaging with a brand new customer for the first time he/she doesn't necessarily need to do extensive formal research first.

Just to be clear, this is not a suggestion that you should avoid doing your homework on a particular market sector or customer. It's simply an acknowledgement that B2B companies are learning organisations,[9] and typically their employees already have a lot of prior knowledge about their sector and its customers. This knowledge enables what is called in the research of Aron O'Cass of Newcastle Business School and Liem Viet Ngo of the University of New South Wales in Australia a 'pre-emptive strategic value offering'. They explain this in 'Examining the firm's value creation process: A managerial perspective of the firm's value offering strategy and performance, *British Journal of Management*, Vol. 22, 646–671. This ability echoes the suggestion by Dixon and Adamson that sales professionals should be teachers who use their market knowledge to bring provocative new insights to customers about their market sector.

A pre-emptive value offer is the ability to have a pretty good idea in advance about what value looks like in a particular market sector. From this point of view B2B sales executives are recognised as 'intelligent observers' of the market within which they operate and who are able to competently infer what will be valued by a customer where an industry outsider or novice can't. Basically, seasoned B2B sales professionals have a lot of experience which means they intuitively know how to provide distinctive and personal customer value through their knowledge, expertise and a positive relational experience. This in turn means that the experienced B2B sales executive is able, in advance, to form a clear and broadly accurate idea about what the customer will value, even though the customer will ultimately be the judge and creator of value through use of a product or service.

Two key things are important here. First, we should emphasise that sales professionals have a responsibility back to the business to ensure this knowledge is passed on to the rest of organisation through marketing.

Too many books make it look as if market analysis starts from ground zero even though there is all this latent sales knowledge on tap! We call acting on this experience being able to make 'pre-emptive value judgements' that result in creating a pre-emptive value perspective that aligns and balances the following:

---

[9] The learning organisation and organisational learning are ideas about how market knowledge is used in businesses. See the work of Peter Senge in his book *The Fifth Discipline* and the work of Chris Argyris in his book *On Organizational Learning*.

- Commercial value for the customer
- Commercial value for the supplier
- Reputational value for the supplier
- Relational value for both parties

The ability to simultaneously hold different types of value in mind demonstrates that the sales executive is able to balance the commercial needs of the supplier and the customer, nurture relational value from the moment of first contact onwards and recognise reputational value in being seen to work with the most esteemed clients and avoiding controversy.

- Commercial value to the customer includes improved profitability, help to compete and providing a capability to go to market faster, as we saw in Chap. 2.
- Commercial value to the supplier includes continuity of purchase, improved profitability, early involvement in customers' plans.
- Relational value includes access to onward suppliers and markets, access to confidential insights and information, preferential treatment.
- Reputational value includes being seen to work with well-known brands, being known for making wise commercial judgements, being regarded as an innovator and thought leader. It also includes protecting reputation in the way that major sports brands cancel sponsorship deals with sportsmen and women caught up in drug scandals.

Being Good at Understanding the Social Dimensions of Buying Situations

We mentioned above Erving Goffman's idea of drama. Using this idea we can imagine customer interactions as if they take place on a theatrical stage. The transactions and relationships between the supplier and customer are acted out on this stage, where the phases of customer interaction are linked just as different scenes of a play or movie are. Seen in this way B2B sales executives are performers with an innate instinct for understanding what is going on behind the scenes of the buying process. This means they are much more than technical experts mechanically managing their way along each step of the analysis and decision-making plan and buying process. Sales professionals show an artful ability to read social situations and perform in the right way. Our research has shown that experienced sales professionals intuitively

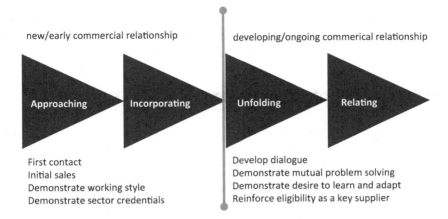

new/early commercial relationship   developing/ongoing commerical relationship

Approaching   Incorporating   Unfolding   Relating

First contact
Initial sales
Demonstrate working style
Demonstrate sector credentials

Develop dialogue
Demonstrate mutual problem solving
Demonstrate desire to learn and adapt
Reinforce eligibility as a key supplier

Fig. 3.1 Social contexts of supplier–seller interaction: Johnston (2014)

recognise four distinct phases of customer interaction, which fall into two early and two later stages of the commercial relationship (Fig. 3.1).

Approaching is the phase of initial customer contact. The point at which a customer notices a need and potential suppliers. *Incorporating* is where the supplier has been invited to do some initial business with the customer. These phases are about the supplier and customer getting to know each other. *Unfolding* is the phase where the customer and supplier start sharing ideas and commercially sensitive information with each other. There is regular contact over time and trust is growing. *Relating* is where the eligibility and credibility of the salesperson have been firmly established in the mind of the customer; there is a close understanding between both parties and regular business being done.

It should be noted that the eligibility and credibility of the supplier is continuously being assessed in every context. This could be lost at any moment through lack of service or poor-quality products. Some mistakes might be forgiven in the contexts of unfolding and relating, but if they continue or are commercially catastrophic then of course everything breaks down.

These scenes can be combined with buying and relationship process models such as the loyalty ladder (Christopher et al. 1991) and a range of buying process models. The loyalty ladder shows how a customer starts the relationship on the bottom rung of a metaphorical relationship ladder and undertakes a transaction with the supplier; then the customer becomes a regular buyer and eventually becomes a partner and an advocate. Jobber and Lancaster's (2014) buying decision process model, taking just one example, describes how customers become aware of a need, then review alternatives and eventually make a choice These models typically describe buyer types and behaviours as they occur in a step-by-step process. The scenes of interaction, however, describe the social *context* in which these types and behaviours occur.

The Four Scenes of Buyer -Seller Interaction

Approaching is the opening scene of the supplier–buyer interaction. Experienced salespeople approach this scene carefully and typically frame the approach as opening a conversation rather than selling. It is the opposite of a cold sales pitch. The key impression to give here is that it must not be hectoring, intrusive or time wasting, and must be positioned to give a strong sense of sector relevance and potential customer value of both the solution and the person making the offer.

Incorporating is the phase where the supplier and the customer are tentatively judging each other's personal credibility. Each party seeks to establish knowledgeability, authority and authenticity. Any lack of sector knowledge needs to be avoided, and an experienced and mature impression is reinforced by informed commercially orientated 'business talk', ideally showing deep market sector understanding using appropriate sector jargon. When credibility and eligibility are established the buyer will 'incorporate' the supplier into his/her world of potential and actual suppliers. The supplier becomes part of the buyer's network.

Unfolding is a phase of mutual openness and discovery, where dialogue takes place between the two parties. It is a situation that facilitates an understanding of what everyone means about prevailing business issues, with open development of thoughts and ideas. The key flavour of this scene is exploratory. Unfolding represents the opportunity to ask questions, engage in reciprocal meaning-making and co-create solutions (Varey 2003; Ballantyne et al. 2011). Candour is also very important in this scene. Participants speak openly and freely, and share confidences and confidential information. Conversation is encouraged and attempts to actively persuade the customer of the benefits of a particular product or service are avoided. If the norms and values of this scene are misread or transgressed by either party, the value of the relationship is considerably reduced. Therefore the supplier is not expected to be dogmatic and manipulative, the customer is not expected to be dogmatic and reticent, and neither party is expected to be deceptive.

Relating is where ongoing relational value is co-created. Experienced salespeople clearly distinguish between the utopian ideals and warm language of relationship marketing and commercial reality. Whilst a relational disposition is something to be appreciated, the hard-nosed aims and purpose of the supplier organisation are not to be overlooked. The understated aim of the salesperson's creation of relational value is of course to make a sale. In this scene of interaction the supplier begins to think and act as if the customer's' business is their business, offering ideas and suggestions for how the customer can shape the market sector they are in.

The crucial thing to realise here is that for each customer there are unique ways of conducting oneself in each scene. What works with one customer (such as familiarity and humour) won't work with another. For example, being informal and familiar at the prospecting stage might work for some customers and be a complete no-no for others.

Goffman (1983) called how we are expected to behave in different scenes of the drama 'orders of interaction'. These are the unwritten, commonly understood rules of appropriate conduct. Some people are very aware and sensitive to these and others are far less perceptive and socially aware. It is often inexperienced and script-focused salespeople who transgress orders of interaction, such as failing to respect other people's time, embarrassing the customer by showing up their lack of knowledge (potentially catastrophic if challenging the customer is done in a clumsy way), criticising the customer's judgement or making poor jokes. At other times new people entering the scene can alter the social dynamics and completely change the expectations and tone of the situation. These scenes of interaction are not just academic theories. They reflect the real world of business as it is experienced by real customer-facing professionals. Here is an example.

A major high street retailer used the services of a three dimensional visualisation company to plan new store layouts. The key account manager of the visualisation company had a long and friendly relationship with the architects and design team of the retailer. Both parties saw themselves in a client relationship and so the working relationship was open and friendly, and one where future plans and ideas were shared. The social context of interaction was clearly one of *unfolding*. In one of the regular account meetings things were proceeding as usual when the buying director turned up unannounced, stopped the conversation and demanded a pitch presentation from the key account manager. The social setting of the meeting instantly shifted from a mutual exploration of ideas to one where the key account was expected to produce an initial value proposition on the spot. The social context of *unfolding* was shifted to the context of *approaching* in an instant. This created a highly embarrassing situation because it wasn't expected and there was no time for preparation. The design team was cowed into silence by the purchasing director and the productivity of the meeting was cancelled out. Whether this was a deliberately disruptive technique on behalf of the buyer is unknown. What is clear that the norms and expectations of the original meeting were clearly transgressed.

The Importance of Dialogue

Service dominant logic highlights the fact that value creation is an ongoing process, something that many B2B professionals would regard as the rather obvious. What this means is that the creation and presentation of value propositions are no longer exclusively associated with a particular moment at the early stage of customer contact and are no longer entirely as David Ballantyne et al. (2011) describe it 'supplier crafted'. Value propositions actually emerge and evolve over the course of the developing customer relationship.

The key mechanism that allows this to happen is dialogue. Of course academic concern with communication and value creation during service interactions is not new, as Christian Gronroos (2012) points out:

> Value creation in such interactive contexts was studied as early as the 1970s in the early days of modern service marketing research.

The recent interest in dialogue represents a shift from the historical one-way supplier to customer communication that has been the primary focus of marketing management and mass advertising for decades. Richard Varey (2003) points out that this one-way or monologic type of communication does little for facilitating open and trusting relationships. Monologic communication is characterised by *saying* rather than *listening*, and is associated with one person trying to exert power over the other through persuasion rather than collaboration.

Richard Varey stresses that dialogue is not simply sending a message and getting some feedback; it is a process of two parties working towards a new position of understanding such that, as Christian Gronroos says, each party comes to know the part it plays in the value creation processes of the other.

Dialogue is therefore essential in understanding value systems and value processes of both the supplier and the customer. Dialogue is a:

> method of inquiry and a process of change that occurs when people speak with and listen to one another in mutuality, reciprocity, and co-inquiry thus changing their shared reality. Hazen (1994: 396)

It is from this perspective that Ballantyne et al. (2011: 205) suggest that the co-creation of value 'logically begins with reciprocal value propositions', which are dependent on the need for dialogue and knowledge-sharing in a process of interactive learning. Crucial in this conceptualisation of value proposition is the shift from seeing communication as transfer undertaken by transmitters (cf. Shannon and Weaver (1949) *Mathematical Theory of Communication*) to communication as process.

Christian Kowalkowski of Linkoping University, Sweden, in his 2011 article 'Dynamics of value propositions: Insights from service dominant logic', concludes that value propositions are thus temporary and fluid constructions, not 'frozen' entities; they need to be dynamic to reflect (a) the current version of value held by the customer and (b) the status and time frame of the relationship between the supplier and customer. In this way the interaction and creation of propositions between supplier and customer

> … are not 'show and tell' sessions but back and forth conversations between people who are trying to arrive at the same point together. Miller et al. (2012: 1)

Seems like the purchasing director of the high street retailer mentioned above was an expert in destroying value!

So how do real world executives describe this back-and-forth conversation and the dialogue that takes place to unlock customer value? Here's what some of the people we interviewed said.

Gail, who works for an enterprise software sales business, told us how she worked with clients to unlock value through conversations:

> …we decided we're going to do a discovery meeting and just talk it through and see … they would normally be known as workshops rather than an away day.

Colin, who worked for a major business lending bank, told us how lack of dialogue disrupts any chance of making progress in unlocking customer value:

> it's strange that someone would entertain a meeting if they're not interested in talking otherwise why bother having it. So if they're showing little enthusiasm then you're thinking well why are you bothering?

Sophie, who worked for a university research and product development centre, emphasised the role she played in being the critical friend to the customer to unlock customer value:

> They trust me. I challenge them. But I also hopefully help them. Because they've had a lot of significant improvements through doing development programmes with us.

Ian, CEO of an office refit and refurbishment business, summed up the whole idea of unlocking customer value through having customer dialogue as:

> It's clocking time together, isn't it? It's flying hours, as it were.

Time matters in the process of unlocking B2B value. Re-set the relationship clock and you are actually re-setting the value that has been accrued over time.

Being Good at Understanding What Is Relevant to the Customer

Being relevant to the customer seems like yet another one of those things that is so obvious it hardly deserves a mention. Several authors have written about the need to be relevant in sales and marketing, such as David Aaker (2011), who talks about brand relevance, and Andrea Coville (2014), who talks about how relevance can be used to create competitive advantage. But what do we actually mean by saying something is *relevant*?

We believe that the idea of relevance is essential to understanding value in use because it brings together several things we have discussed:

- Only customers can select what is relevant to them
- Relevance can change over time
- Relevance depends on the customer context
- Understanding the relevance of something depends on dialogue
- Understanding relevance depends on experienced and informed interpretation by the salesperson

Relevance-making is, we believe, a vital and hitherto taken for granted capability that is foundational to value-ology. It is the B2B to salesperson's ability to recognise and understand what is relevant to the customer and understand the relevance of the potential supplier solutions that makes a telling difference to the process of unlocking value. It is a vital aspect of high-quality customer feedback into the marketing strategy process.

Relevance Contextualises Customer Benefits

Most sales and marketing professionals are familiar with the term customer benefit, and use of the word benefit is pervasive in all aspects of sales and marketing activity. Transforming features into benefits is the *raison d'être* of everyday sales and marketing activity. We are all implored by textbooks and consultants to 'sell the benefits'. So, rather than describe what something *is*, such as a cell phone's memory size and its operating system, as sales and marketing professionals we are trained to explain what the solution will *do* for the customer, such as organise your time or help you find a place to eat in a strange town. In the consumer world our products will make you happy; in the business world our solutions will help you compete, get to market faster or make more money.

We believe that the language of *benefit* inadvertently locks sales and marketing professionals into the idea that value is pre-given by the supplier and exchanged rather than co-created. The idea of relevance adds to this traditional way of understanding products and services by emphasising the process of continual value sense, checking to unlock how the customer determines what they regard as a benefit in the first place.

Relevance-making is something that informs the pre-emptive value calls that salespeople make about customer value but does not determine what that value truly is, because only the customer can do that. Relevance-making allows the salesperson to engage in proposing value without going as far as being pushy and presumptive and trying to tell the customer what value is.

The issue of relevance-making was brought home by Eric, the CEO of a national facilities management company, when he told us:

> Now if we're not careful and we keep just cookie cutting the same thing out, without ever taking a step away with the client to say is it still relevant, the ultimate worst case scenario is that the property director of the customer sees somebody else's work and says wow, that's really sexy and current, I'll talk to them 'cause my suppliers aren't adding any value to this process.

With this case in mind we might paraphrase Ted Levitt's famous statement in his 1980 *Harvard Business Review* article 'Marketing success through the differentiation of anything', where he refers to suppliers who are offering something that is meaningfully different as instead 'offering something that is *relevant*'. Only the customer can select what is relevant to them.

Relevance-making is inextricably linked to how people notice things that are new and different. As soon as we become aware of something that gets our attention, we immediately try and work out its relevance to us. This is a deep psychological instinct that originally helped early man decide if something was a threat to life or something that could enhance it. Billy Clark from Middlesex University in London in his book *Relevance Theory* (2013) says:

> as we look, listen to and perceive the world we are looking for relevance.

In more everyday language, software systems account manager Monica told us about how she understood purchasing managers qualifying of contact approaches:

> they're trying to cut out the rubbish and that's the way they do it.

What this means is that relevance is the way in which customers select suppliers. Back in 1912 Schiller defined relevance in his article similarly titled 'Relevance':

> Relevance is the product not an attempt to include everything, but of an effort to get rid of the rubbish, to select the humanly valuable part, and to exclude, reject and ignore the rest... The 'relevant,' therefore, stands out of a chaotic whole as a selected extract.

In modern marketing language, relevance is what customers use to cut through the noise from the multitude of suppliers clamouring for their attention and identify value proposals that are meaningfully different. Alf, the CEO of an industrial window manufacturer, described to us how he handles initial supplier approaches:

> When the value offer gets through to me, then it would be to do with whatever at that moment is going to add value to the company, my customer or the shareholder, it has to add value, to do something.

We can characterise the special nature of relevance as follows:
Customer's relevance selectivity:

- It either is or it isn't
- The offer relates to the matter in hand
- The offer is functional

To re-emphasise the point, the supplier cannot impose relevance on the customer. The customer will determine relevance in the following way:

It Is or It Isn't This means that customers judge if the proposed solution and or the salesperson has value or not. There is no halfway house where the customer thinks 'that's almost relevant to what I need'.

Related to Matter in Hand This means that the value proposal made by the supplier has to be related to a significant matter in hand; in that sense it needs to be sensitive to context by being topical and pertinent to a specific problem or issue, not vague. It also allows the supplier to demonstrate market sector knowledge and professional expertise and specialism. The customer's matter in hand might be an immediate crisis or a long term strategic concern.

Functional This means the proposal has the evident potential to achieve commercial or aspirational goals (it is a means to an end), which in turn requires a clear grasp of the customer's priorities, which can only be known through dialogue.

In summary, for the customer the value proposition and proposer need to signal to the customer that the proposition contains, as Sperber and Wilson (2012) define it, 'information worth having'.

Relevance focuses our attention on what is the matter in hand in the customer's world: what is pressing, and what is strategically important.

Using Relevance-Making Capability to Build Value-Ology

We can model each of the essential aspects of relevance-making capability that are used to unlock customer value. It needs to be borne in mind that these are not 'techniques' as such but more the style and tone of conducting supplier–customer interaction at the social level.

Relevance-making capability:

- Context aware
- Generated through dialogue
- Sensitive to selectivity
- Interprets and connects issues and information

Context Aware Means that the supplier realises that the particular circumstances and what the customer values can change at any moment. Understanding customer context means understanding the customer's 'matter in hand'.

Sensitive to Selectivity Means the supplier cannot impose his/her version of what value means on the customer. Should this be done it is likely to break the orders of interaction and create the impression of being impolite and untrustworthy.

Generated Through Dialogue Means that unless an open and candid sharing of views and priorities takes place a true mutual and reciprocal understanding of value cannot be achieved.

Interprets and Connects Means that definitions of value and relevance need to be interpreted because value is subjective. Connections need to be made between the nature of the customer's problem and aspirations and the potential solutions the supplier can offer.

The notion of relevance-making offers the possibility of reframing the way in which suppliers think about *the* ideas of differentiation and customer benefit. Attention to relevance ensures the actor remains in tune with things that are currently of value, things that are not relevant any more and things that have a chance of becoming relevant in the future.

The Arts of Value-Ology

We describe the act of unlocking customer value as the performing art of the value-proposing professional. This performing art is a vital aspect of value-ology. By emphasising the performance of the sales professional we mean to draw attention to his/her social skill and abilities. This is in contrast to being concerned with how he/she manages the steps of the buying process and uses persuasive sales techniques. These are the essential aspects of their artful performance.

Arts of the value-proposing professional:

- Acting
- Seeing
- Speaking

Acting refers to the way in which sales professionals behave. They are socially intelligent and aware of the situation they are in, they balance a range of stakeholder views on value, and propose rather than persuade by displaying possibilities and alternatives.

Seeing refers to the way in which sales professionals make sense of the customer's world. They connect the customer's problems with solutions, they explore possibilities for adaptation and can imagine how things might look that are currently absent and need creating.

Speaking refers to the way in which sales professionals communicate. They encourage dialogue through relational behaviours such as trust, politeness and honesty. They develop conversations rather than attempting to cajole and persuade, and they facilitate new understandings.

Conclusion

We have introduced the idea that the concepts of value proposition and how value is proposed by the supplier come together as the art of the value-proposing professional. The value-proposing professional demonstrates the valuable and valued social capabilities that are necessary for the on-going process of proposing and unlocking a customer. This is the art of value-ology. The key take here is that *how* the value proposition is communicated to the customer matters as much as the commercial characteristics of the proposition itself.

Steve Murray, entrepreneur and Chairman of UK-based electronic games company Storm Gaming, pointed out that we make personal value judgements within seconds of a first meeting. He described to us that in his view the value-proposing professional is a persuasive diplomat: a person who pays attention to their personal appearance, attire and behaviours, someone who simultaneously informs and listens, someone who pays authentic and attentive interest to the person they are talking to. These people continually sense-check their propositions for relevance and adapt their style and approach to the customer, making them feel as if they are the absolute focus of attention. He described the value-proposing professional as the social glue that held the company's offer and what the customer was looking for from a supplier together.

Sales professionals are clearly a valuable competitive difference.[10] This is not just because they know and can access a customer base. The social capabilities they have are not spread equally across everyone who engages in customer interactions. In that sense the capabilities of the value-proposing professional can be called dynamic capabilities.[11] Such capabilities differentiate companies in situations where customers and markets are hard to predict and change-

---

[10] Kathleen Eisenhardt and Jeffrey Martin noted in their article 'Dynamic capabilities: What are they?', *Strategic Management Journal*; Oct/Nov 2000; 21, 10/11 that a superior sales force was a main plank of value creating strategies.

[11] The idea of dynamic capabilities was originally put forward by David Teece.

able, and where knowledge and insight can be used to manage change in the business environment, adapting resources inside the company to meet customer needs.

Activity

Customer value is unlocked when value in use is created. This happens through the impression the salesperson gives to the customer and how the salesperson reads what is going on during customer interactions. It is essential to ensuring that the salesperson is taken seriously by the customer.

Exercise: What must we do to ensure our customers take us seriously as value-proposing professionals?
Think about a particular customer.

- Using what you have learned above, map out the do's and don'ts that are relevant to the phase of social interaction with the customer.
- Give your take on pre-emptive value by stating the relevant matter at hand for the customer in each social interaction phase, and what makes you distinctive (Fig. 3.2)

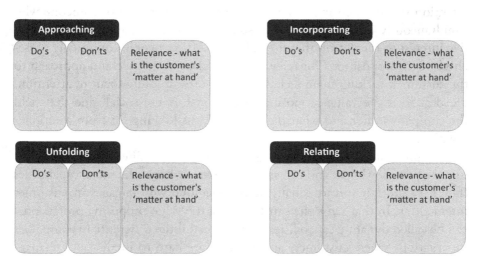

Fig. 3.2   Mapping the social contexts of customer interaction

Discuss the implications of this analysis with colleagues.

Is anything missing from your market and customer knowledge?

Are any changes needed in your way of working to be taken seriously by your customers, in order to unlock value?

Further Reading

Clark T, Salaman G. (1998). Creating the 'right' impression: Towards a dramaturgy of management consultancy. *The Service Industries Journal, 18*(1), 18–38.

Varey, R. (2003) A dialogical foundation for marketing. *The Marketing Review 2*, 273–288.

References

Aaker, D. (2011). *Brand relevance: Making competitors irrelevant*. San Francisco: Wiley.

Bagozzi, R. P. (2006). The role of social and self-conscious emotions in the regulation of business to business relationships in salesperson-customer interactions. *Journal of Business Marketing, 21*(7), 459–457.

Baumann, J., & Le Meunier-FitzHugh, K. (2015). Making value co-creation a reality – Exploring the co-creative value processes in customer–salesperson interaction. *Journal of Marketing Management, 31*(3–4), 289–316.

Ballantyne, D., & Varey, R. J. (2006). Creating value-in-use through marketing interaction: The exchange logic of relating, communicating and knowing. *Marketing Theory, 6*(3), 335–348.

Ballantyne, D., Frow, P., Varey, R. J., & Payne, A. (2011). Value propositions as communication practice: Taking the wider view. *Industrial Marketing Management, 40*, 202–210.

Blocker, C. P., Cannon, J. P., Panagopoulos, N. G., & Sager, J. K. (2012). The role of the sales force in value creation and appropriation: New directions for research. *Journal of Personal Selling & Sales Management, 32*(1), 15–27.

Christopher, M., Payne, A., & Ballantyne, D. (1991). *Relationship marketing. Bringing quality, customer service and marketing together*. Oxford: Butterworth-Heinemann.

Cialdini, R.B. (2000). *Influence: Science and practice* (4th ed.). Pearson Education - USA: Allyn & Bacon.

Clark, B. (2013). *Relevance theory*. New York: Cambridge University Press.

Clark, T., & Salaman, G. (1998). Creating the 'right' impression: Towards a dramaturgy of management consultancy. *The Service Industries Journal, 18*(1), 18–38.

Coville, A. (2014). *Relevance: The power to change minds and behavior and stay ahead of the competition.* Brookline: Bibliomotion Incorporated.

Dixon, M., & Adamson, B. (2011). *The challenger sale. Taking control of the customer conversation.* New York: Portfolio-Penguin.

Goffman, E. (1983). The interaction order. *American Sociological Review, 48*(1), 1–17.

Goffman, E. (1990). *The presentation of self in everyday life.* UK: Penguin.

Gronroos, C. (2000). *Service management and marketing: A customer relationship management approach.* New York: Wiley.

Gronroos, C. (2012). Conceptualising value co-creation: A journey to the 1970s and back to the future. *Journal of Marketing Management, 28*(13–14), 1520–1534.

Guenzi, P., Pardo, C., & Georges, L. (2007). Relational selling strategy and key account managers' relational behaviors: An exploratory study. *Industrial Marketing Management, 36*(1), 121–133.

Hazen, M. A. (1994). A radical humanist perspective of inter organisational relationships. *Human Relations, 47*(4), 393–415.

Hogan, K. (1996). *The psychology of persuasion: How to persuade others to your way of thinking* (1st ed.). USA: Pelican Publishing.

Jobber, D., & Lancaster, G. (2014). *Selling and sales management* (9th ed.). UK: Prentice Hall.

Johnston, P.R. (2014). Proposing business to business customer value: Towards understanding the value proposing actor. Doctoral thesis. Sheffield Business School. Sheffield Hallam University. United Kingdom.

Kowalkowski, C. (2011). Dynamics of value propositions: Insights from service-dominant logic. *European Journal of Marketing, 45*(1/2), 277–294.

Levitt, T. (1980). Marketing success through the differentiation of anything. *Harvard Business Review, 58*(1), 83–91.

Miller, R.B., Heiman, S.E., & Tuleja, T. (2005). *The new strategic selling* (Rev Upd ed.). USA: Business Plus.

Miller, R.B., Heiman, S.E., & Tuleja, T. (2012). *The new conceptual selling* (2nd ed.). UK: Kogan Page.

O'Cass, A., & Ngo, L. V. (2011). Examining the firm's value creation process: A managerial perspective of the firm's value offering strategy and performance. *British Journal of Management, 22*, 646–671.

Payne, A., Christopher, M., Peck, H., & Clark, M. (1998). *Relationship marketing for competitive advantage.* Oxford: Butterworth- Heinemann.

Pink, D.H. (2012). *To sell is human.* Canongate.

Rackham, N. (1995). *SPIN selling.* Gower.

Schiller, F.C.S. (1912). Relevance. *Mind, 21*(82), 153–166, Oxford University.

Shannon, C. E., & Weaver, W. (1949). *Mathematical theory of communication.* Urbana: University of Illinois Press.

Shostack, G.L. (1977) Breaking free from product marketing, Journal of Marketing 41(2): 73–80.

Sperber, D., & Wilson, D. (2012). *Meaning and relevance*. UK: Cambridge University Press.

Stevenson, R.L. (1892). *Across the plains with other memories and essays*. London: Chatto and Windus Piccadilly. Accessed via https://ia600303.us.archive.org/28/items/with00stevacrossplainsrich/

Varey, R. J. (2003). A dialogical foundation for marketing. *The Marketing Review, 3*, 273–288.

Vargo, S. L., & Lusch, R. F. (2011). It's all B2B…And beyond. Towards as systems perspective of the market. *Industrial Marketing Management, 40*, 181–187.

Williams, A. J., & Seminerio, J. (1985). What buyers like from salesmen. *Industrial Marketing Management, 14*, 75–78.

Part 2

Creating Your Value-ology Blueprint

4

Unearthing Customer Value

In this chapter we will look at:

- Why a theme-based approach to value propositions is beneficial
- How to get to the key themes and issues affecting your customers
- Understanding what drives change (Industry themes versus individual customer issues)
- The mixed method approach to gathering customer intelligence
- Tips to get the most out of customer interviews
- Final thoughts

Identifying what your customers need and want from your company is not always as easy as it sounds. Common sense would tell you just to ask your customers, but they may be unaware that they have a problem or that possibilities exist to solve their problem. The secret lies in your ability to ask the right questions, read and analyse data, and ultimately connect the dots for your customer. As we saw in Chap. 3, excellent sales teams have the essential capabilities that are needed to discover the issues and problems that really matter to the customer and give an experienced interpretation of what is going on at account level. It is essential, therefore, that the sales team is included very early on in value proposition development meetings and conversations to make sure the real depth of customer value understanding is captured.

In this chapter we will discuss why a theme-based approach will improve the success of your marketing and sales efforts, and how to develop themes that will resonate with your target audience. As this should be an ongoing

© The Author(s) 2017
S. Kelly et al., *Value-ology*,
DOI 10.1007/978-3-319-45626-3_4

effort, we will also share some ideas on how to stay on top of the issues affecting your customers.

If we go back to the value proposition stack we introduced in Chap. 2 (Fig. 2.1) we see that at the top of the stack the aim is to develop customer value propositions (CVPs) tailored to individuals. To hit all the right notes and resonate with your customer, a value proposition should be MUSICAL:

Monetary calculation—of financial benefits minus costs
Unique—things that set you apart from competitors
Spend (costs)—how much the customer is prepared to pay
Impact—how it will positively impact the customer organisation
Capability—what it is that you can do for the customer to make this impact
ALigned—to the key needs of the customer

These types of value propositions are really the climax of the 'whole system' approach to value we are putting forward. Like Webster (2002) we believe that value propositions should be the 'single most important organizing principle' for companies. This approach is based on a deep level of customer understanding. So, lots of work is required at the lower levels of the value stack to put you in a position to develop MUSICAL value propositions.

We can see that most of the elements of the term MUSICAL are about the customer, as we would expect them to be. The Unique and Capability elements are related to your own organisation. This necessarily means that you need good understanding of the customer and their industry combined with a good understanding of your own company to develop compelling value propositions.

The flow of this chapter will follow the value proposition stack from bottom to top to give you a view of the research required at each level. This will begin with developing an understanding of the key customer business issues leading to the development of proposition themes. Before we do this, let's remind ourselves why developing overarching proposition themes is important.

The Benefits of a Theme-Based Approach

In Chap. 2 we saw that the key benefits of a theme-based approach are:

- To demonstrate to the customer through all your communications that you are trying to make a difference or add value to their business

- To provide a discipline that uses customer issues as a starting point for all your conversations
- To ensure that you are not bombarding customers with irrelevant, disjointed messages, that jump from product to product
- To save marketing money, as you can array all your products and solutions under these themes
- To make more money, as in our experience if you use this approach you don't have a cross-sell, up-sell problem since you are not selling one product at a time

The themes that you select should:

- Capture the essence of the key customer issues that you feel your company can address
- Resonate with customers as something they are aspiring to achieve and are relevant to them
- Be broad and flexible enough to allow sector, segment and customer tailoring as you move up the value stack towards financially justified individual CVPs

Why Creating Themes Matters

Themes are a way of organising customer communications and solutions into an overarching big idea that will resonate with customers because of the theme links to key issues they face. This provides a platform for you to communicate and demonstrate that you understand the essence of their business problems and provide solutions for them. In Chap. 5 we will see how themes can help us think creatively about blending together individual products or services into solutions.

Theme creation is part art, part science and relies on the skill and market knowledge of the sales and marketing team. The particular thinking skill that is used is called 'chunking'.[1] Chunking is basically a hierarchy of categories where the theme is the top of the hierarchy and things that are deemed to belong to the theme sit below it. To create a theme we 'chunk up' from

---

[1] Chunking is an idea originally proposed by John Grinder and Richard Bandler. It refers to how people categorise things in their mind. People with an eye for detail focus on small chunks and people who look at the big picture focus on big chunks. Big chunks are always made of small chunks. The motor industry is a big chunk; Chrysler, Ford, Toyota are smaller chunks that make up the big chunk. See the work of Bertrand Russell and Gregory Bateson on the theory of logical types for a more detailed exposition.

individual distinct solutions under the customer themes. A similar approach is used in creating a brand. Brands are frequently umbrellas that contain diverse products within them, such as Ford or Kellogg's.

The work of Professor Sam Ham on thematic interpretation (1992, 2005) shows that if you want to make a difference to the people you are communicating with and you want people to internalise and remember what you said, you should use a theme. This is because people are initially overwhelmed with details and forget them, whereas they remember themes. This is becoming an ever more difficult challenge because of the explosion of content that customers are being exposed to. Studies show that we are bombarded with anything from 500 to 5000 calls on our attention a day.[2]

Sam Ham's work helps us cut through this noise by quickly and easily communicating to the customer about the big picture; why it is relevant to them and why it's a big deal. Of course, as we pointed out in Chap. 2, there are pitfalls to avoid. The biggest potential pitfall is picking themes that are too generic and do not resonate. The second is picking restrictive themes that do not allow wiggle room to add different contexts as you move up the value proposition stack.

How to Identify Key Proposition Themes

A key upside that Sam Ham attributes to developing themes is that it unlocks creativity. This is something we wholeheartedly agree with. The way you approach analysing and interpreting data is what can set you apart, even if the data is available to your competitors. Spotting a unique theme or pattern that resonates with customers can give you a proprietary advantage. If you are the first to the theme and you use it systematically, as we advocate, you could be seen by the customers as 'owning' the theme. Coca-Cola and 'happiness', Microsoft and 'productivity', Apple and 'simplicity', IBM and 'lowering risk in an uncertain world' are examples that spring to mind.

To stick with our theme of themes we recommend that you follow the principles of thematic analysis. This is a research method for identifying, analysing and reporting patterns (themes) within data (Braun and Clarke 2006). It involves searching for repetitive themes that occur across data. Here we are eating our own dog food: our own research outlined in Chaps. 3 and 9 involved thematic analysis.

---

[2] See K. Rhoads (1997) *Everyday Influence in Working Psychology* for a seminal study of information overload.

Many people in business research roles intuitively use this kind of approach. In simple terms you need to gather enough data to arrive at a point where you see recurring or interesting themes. You don't have to select the ones that occur most. Pick themes that are clearly impacting on your customer base and lead to products you can sell that fix the problems inherent in the themes. It's also a good idea to pick a theme that's reasonably enduring through changing contexts so you're not chopping and changing all the time. For example, 'Agility' and 'Customer Delight' are themes that can endure through recessionary times as well as for periods of strong economic growth. The context of the topic for the different context is important here. 'Why Agility can help you survive these tough times' would resonate in a recession, while 'Delighting Customers to stay ahead of the growth curve' would be relevant in better economic conditions.

In-short, a theme should:

- Be grounded in business issues
- Resonate with your customers
- Lead to solutions that you can sell to help with the issues
- Be enduring
- Be able to accommodate topics and products to maximise the theme impact

In Chap. 9 we go into marketing and sales alignment in some depth. Selecting the themes could be seen to be largely a marketing activity. It would make sense to ask sales for input about what they are observing in the marketplace and to use any relevant data they may have in your customer relationship management system. Assuming the sales people currently talk to customers about the issues they face, of course.

So how do you know the difference between important, business-driving, themes and interesting but non-actionable themes? We are often asked this, and the answer is in the question. If the potential theme cannot lead towards something your organisation can sell to help customers move forward, then cross it off the list. There are three factors that can help you with your choice:

- Impact: how big an impact is this issue or theme likely to have on your customer base?
- Urgency: how urgent is it? If there is some impending legislation that is going to affect your customers then it may be something that should influence theme selection
- Size of opportunity: what sort of opportunity could this offer your organisation?

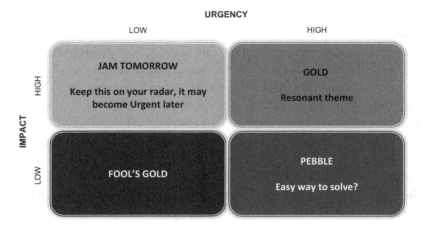

Fig. 4.1 Impact urgency opportunity model

What you're aiming for is something that is high impact and high urgency for customers. Crucially, once you've found something that fits these criteria it needs to be a big opportunity for you. You can visually array potential themes on the four box model in Fig. 4.1 to help give you a sense of priority, and ultimately assist you in picking a resonant customer theme that will impact your bottom line, as well as theirs.

The Mixed Method Approach to Gathering Customer Intelligence

Now that we've established the importance of a theme-based approach, how do you go about gathering this level of customer intelligence?

You may be familiar with different types of research methods below—each designed to collect different types of data.

- *Secondary Research*, also known as desk research, involves gathering existing data that has already been produced. Examples of secondary data include reports and studies by government agencies, trade associations or other businesses within your industry, researching the internet, newspapers and company reports. Some of these sources are free and in the public domain. Others have either a subscription service or may ask for a one-off fee to buy a piece of research.
- Confusingly you should perform secondary research first. Look for what's out there. We don't regard it as heretical to say this but there may be enough

available to give you a very good start for your theme development. We've already said that proprietary advantage can be gained by interpreting this secondary data in creative ways.

- What you look for and where you look is determined by where your target customer base is. Does it have a global presence? Is it in a particular region? Do you focus on particular types of executives, for example, Chief Information Officers (CIOs)? Key customer issues publications such as *The Economist, Financial Times, Wall Street Journal* and *Harvard Business Review* often feature special reports. Companies such as Gartner and Forrester Research have a particular focus on technology, while *Marketing Week* can provide insights into what's affecting marketers.

- *Primary research*, also known as field research, involves gathering new data that has not been collected before; for example, surveys using question-naires or interviews with groups of people in a focus group. Performing formal primary research can be costly. The secondary research should have helped answer some questions and help you identify gaps in your knowl-edge. You may also see opportunities to gather insights into your customers that could provide you with a useful communication vehicle to involve customers in the primary research sample and to send them your analysis of the output. IBM performs an annual CIO study that follows this pattern and helps put them in a thought leadership position regarding emerging technology issues and trends.

- *Quantitative research* is rooted in numerical approaches. The emphasis is on objectivity and the use of statistics or data gathered through polls, ques-tionnaires or surveys. With quantitative research methods, numerical data are gathered and then generalised across groups of people to explain trends. These methods begin from questions such as 'how many?', 'how often?', 'when?' and 'where?'.

- *Qualitative research* is designed to reveal a target audience's range of behav-iour and the perceptions that drive it with reference to specific topics or issues. If you want to get inside your customers' minds you need to do qualitative research. Face-to-face interviews and focus groups can provide valuable insights into your products, your market and your customers. Qualitative research is about finding out not just what people think but why they think it. It's about getting people to talk about their opinions so you can understand their motivations and feelings. Face-to-face interviews and group discussions are the best way to get this kind of in-depth feedback. Qualitative research can be valuable when you are developing new prod-ucts or coming up with new marketing initiatives and you want to test reactions and refine your approach.

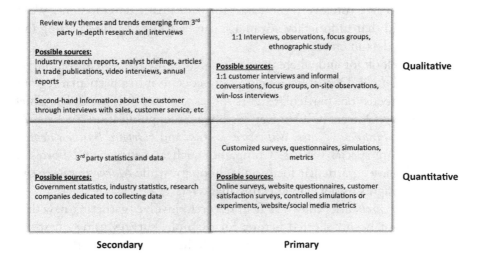

Fig. 4.2 Mixed method approach to gathering customer intelligence

There is no one way to conduct research, and we recommend that you combine a variety of tactics and techniques to ensure that the data you collect is balanced, well rounded and valid.

In fact, in the field of social and behavioural sciences, there is an entire journal named *The Journal of Mixed Methods Research*, which is dedicated to explaining how to design and conduct mixed research methods to better understand problems and inform decisions.

We encourage you to incorporate the sources and methods illustrated in Fig. 4.2 in order to weave together patterns and form a holistic view of your customers' worlds.

Industry Vertical or Segment Research

The mixed methods approach holds good for each level of the value proposition stack. The mix of the methods will vary as you get closer to the customer, as will the nature of the research and the sources. If you selected 'Agility' as one of your top level themes how does this play out at customer segment or sector level? So, for example, what are the major agility challenges in motor manufacturing? What are the key performance indicators they use to measure agility? What other sector-specific issues are there that may fit under this theme?

You may use some of the intelligence from the earlier analysis you performed to get to the themes. Clearly macro factors such as oil prices and global economic conditions will affect motor manufacturers. For specific sector information you may consult industry bodies such as the Society of Motor Manufacturers and Traders or the Retail Motor Industry Federation. There may be professional bodies for people who work in the industry, in this case, the Institute of the Motor Industry.

In every sector there are likely to be analysts and research companies that focus on those sectors. In telecoms and IT (information technology), companies such as Forrester and Gartner provide high-quality sector intelligence. Companies such as Verdict specialise in retail research whilst Mintel provides reports on many fast-moving consumer goods markets.

The nature of the research will also change as the focus starts to be on individual organisations and people. Who are the key movers and shakers in the sector? How well is your organisation connected with them? How do they buy in this sector/segment? These are some of the questions that need to be answered here. It's highly likely that you will want to talk to customers, and to their customers, to develop your own primary research, so that you can publish and communicate your own insight into the sector.

As we move closer to the customer, this industry-level information will help make theme discussions much more relevant and resonant. 'Delighting students in a competitive undergraduate market' would be a subject that would fit the context of the UK education sector right now.

One commercial organisation we worked with used eminent business school professors to help develop provocation papers about industry topics to attract key executives to discuss these issues in round table forums. This had the dual effect of raising contacts levels and improving industry knowledge. Crucially these forums helped leverage some significant sales.

At the sector level the marketing versus sales input equation also changes. The sales guys are out with these customers all the time. Given that they probably specialise in selling to a sector they are likely to know a fair amount about it. Working closely with sales to ensure they are happy with developing sector context around the themes is key here.

Customer and Individual Level Research

Moving to the top two levels of the value proposition stack, it's important that the research has a level of granularity that helps you truly understand whole customer and individual issues. Only by knowing this will you be able to develop truly resonant and relevant CVPs.

At customer level, we need to answer the plea of the financial services C-level executive we met in Chap. 2: 'Don't treat me like any other financial services company, recognize that I have unique issues and challenges.'

The investor relations sections of company websites can provide a rich source of performance data and analysis about individual companies. You will find annual reports and presentations to shareholders here. Some questions to answer when looking at annual reports include:

- What were their major achievements last year?
- What were the biggest issues/challenges they face?
- What are the top initiatives they are focused on this year? (Growth, expansion, client acquisition, building a stronger culture, etc.)
- How do they plan to achieve their goals?

Some of the sources we identified earlier will also provide commentary of individual company performance. The *Financial Times*, *The Economist* and *Wall Street Journal* provide insight into issues and performance for, say, HSBC. Websites such as Investors Chronicle (www.investorschronicle.co.uk) will give you trend and share performance along with commentary on issues affecting the company and its performance. If you set up regular feeds from reputable sources it's amazing what opportunities you can develop.

Here you need to get to a point where you can build value propositions that really resonate; for example, 'XYZ Paints and Coatings company is looking to increase the speed of bringing innovations to market in order to grow revenue and keep its leading industry position.' This is the agility issue for XYZ paints.

The difference at these two levels to what may have gone before is that your research is geared to producing MUSICAL value propositions that help you develop and close sales. In order to do this you will need to understand:

- **M**—how you can arrive at a monetary value of the benefits your solution can deliver
- **U**—what's unique about your offer that can deliver these benefits better than competitors
- **S**—how much the customer is prepared to pay
- **I**—how it will positively impact the customer
- **C**—what capability you have that helps make this impact: this may not just be a product, it could well be a set of skills that you have
- **AL**—what the key customer needs are so that you can develop something that delivers value against these needs

At this stage the skew of sales to marketing input swings heavily. Lots of the calorie burning will have to be done by sales to translate the theme and sector level value propositions into something meaningful not just at a customer level but for the 5.4 (CEB Research) individuals who are typically involved in purchasing. Marketing can usefully help run workshops, as we have, encouraging sales to bring in selections of press clippings about their customers to think about the potential opportunities that can be developed. In one session we ran for a client, the salesperson was able to find out about a security hit on a customer website which occurred on that day. The 'double whammy' for him was that the problem could be resolved by his own company in the shape of a website security offer.

Here the research takes a further shift, and becomes even more about people than it is at sector level. Who are the key people in the account? Do we have a relationship with them? Do any of our senior executives know any of their key players? What issues are they facing? What motivates them, in or out of work.

It is highly likely that sales guys have received training from reputable organisations to help perform this kind of analysis. Understanding who's involved in making decisions, the decision-making process and key influencers in the account are things they know they need to know in order to be successful. At this level marketing needs to help sales successfully tailor value propositions, offers and messages to resonate with the customers. They need to be humble enough to accept that sales is the key player here.

Competitor and Capability Research

To provide context for what we believe is appropriate research here, let's begin by reminding ourselves that this research is to help address the 'Unique' and 'Capability' elements of your MUSICAL value propositions.

It's Not Just About the Product

Many sales and marketing people we talk with, probably north of 60 %, seem to struggle answering this question. One example is the Global Marketing Director for the IT company we met in Chap. 2. He thought his company had an excellent account-based marketing programme, but did not have any sort of competitive advantage because the IT industry is commoditised, in his opinion. We would make two points here. Firstly, we are with Professor Malcolm MacDonald, Emeritus Professor in Marketing, Cranfield, who would say that taking a more customer value-based approach should, in itself, make you unique and give you a level of competitive advantage. Secondly, we already know that research from Forrester suggests that only 16 % of C-level executives bought a solution because of a superior product. So don't be myopic and think of competition as being just at the product level.

Before we talk more about myopia let's consider what we mean by Unique. Well, a dictionary definition is 'the only one of its kind; unlike anything else', and if we try to match up to this definition we may find it tough to hit on something that is truly unique. From what we observe this seems to drive companies to describe what's 'useful' about themselves, from their perspective. Look at company websites or corporate presentations and you see lots of buzz words and blah, blah, blah about 'we have x number of offices, we are best in class, we have the best service, we have y number of employees, our network has z thousand route miles'. OK, you may have more route miles than the next man, but what does this do for the customer?

Just Because You're Unique Doesn't Make You Useful

Here we like to remind ourselves of the maxim 'Just because you're unique doesn't make you useful'. That uniqueness needs to have some utility, or relevance, for the customer. This means it has to be grounded in the things that they say they find valuable, which you should have established from your earlier research.

If they said they were looking to improve productivity you will have presented them with a value proposition that demonstrates how your solution delivered this. Because productivity was important it's likely that one of the key buying criteria was service. Therefore, they would be interested in up-time, repair service response and technical support. In this case your uniqueness should be centred around your ability to deliver the proposed productivity gains through your service capability relating to up-time, response time and technical support. Not much here about the product or the blah, blah, blah route miles. Of course when it gets down to the 'why you' question it could be that the reason you can deliver better response times is because you have lots of locations and engineers near the customer premises, or because you can provide on-site support. There are lots of reasons here to keep the discussion away from price and linked to value.

So, from a competitor intelligence point of view you should be looking through the lens of 'who is competing at the proposition level', competing to deliver the value or benefits. This takes us back to the myopia point.

It's About Competing for Benefits... Proposition Level

In the Preface we made the stark observation that only 48 % of the Fortune 500 at the turn of the millennium are still around in 2016. The seminal Ted Levitt (1960) *Harvard Business Review* article 'Marketing Myopia' urged companies to take a different view of what they were providing to customers—to think about benefits and not products. This approach also helps organisations see competitors through a different lens.

Levitt cited the demise of the US railroads and painted a picture of rail owners looking up to the sky to see short haul flights using their tracks for navigation, while tumbleweed blew through their stations! Levitt's view was that if the railroad owners viewed themselves as in the business of providing transportation and not running railroads they could have foreseen this. At Massachusetts Institute of Technology (MIT), we learned about the demise of the Boston Ice Company, which used to farm ice from Boston Bay, insulate it in ice houses, then ship it around the world. They met their end with the birth of refrigeration, because that was a way more effective method for making food last longer. Again, if Boston Ice Company had viewed itself as delivering solutions that helped people keep their food fresh longer and not a company that farmed ice, its fate might have been different.

Think About New Ways to Deliver the Benefits

With rapidly advancing technology, it's increasingly difficult to see where the competition is coming from. Look at the rise of Airbnb and Uber as completely new business models that have shaken the markets they operate in to the core. So, make sure you have a lens on how new technologies and business models could affect competition in your world, or provide you with new opportunities if you are looking at the world from an eyes-wide-open, benefit standpoint.

Challenge 4.1
So here's the challenge. You may wish to build on work you did in Chap. 2 or start from scratch. With a group of your colleagues discuss and record:

- Examples of companies that have met a similar fate to US railroads and the Boston Ice Company.
- How many of these companies are in your industry?
- What key benefits are your customers looking for you to deliver?
- Who competes with you to deliver these benefits?
- And can you think of some new ways or business models that could emerge to improve the way the benefits could be delivered?
- Could your company develop any of these potential new business models?

Beware: The Most Common Pitfall

If you've worked in the same industry for a while, you may start to get complacent and think you know it all. It's equally tempting to breeze through the research methods outlined in Fig. 4.2 and call it good. But beware, as one of the biggest mistakes we see marketers make is not spending enough time with customers. They often get caught up in the day-to-day aspects of their job, and end up relying on secondhand information *about* their customers rather than first-hand feedback *from* their customers. As one senior marketer put it, filtering feedback from sales and/or product can be valuable, but can often involve some level of bias based on perspective.

Talking directly to customers can lead to valuable insights that you may not have uncovered otherwise. And just because you talked to a few customers last year doesn't mean that things haven't shifted or changed in their world.

Below are four different ways in which you can interact with your customers. We've called these 'levels', as each requires slightly more effort—but the results and intelligence you will gain at each stage are worth it.

Level 1 Interview your customer-facing personnel such as sales, customer service and product management. Listen in on customer phone calls or observe customer meetings. This will help you understand the common triggers and/or patterns that prompt customer inquiries.

Level 2 Conduct your own customer survey, focus group or questionnaire to better understand and quantify their behaviour and attitudes. Interact with customers on social media and reach out to ask questions on Q&A platforms such as Quora and LinkedIn Groups where your customers hang out. Again, pay attention to the words your customer (or prospect) is using. This will help you understand what the biggest areas of focus are so that you can develop messaging and content that resonates and engages with your customers.

Level 3 Conduct one-to-one interviews with your prospects and customers to deepen your knowledge of their motivations, needs and buying criteria. Customer advocacy groups are also a valuable source of information, where you can set the agenda to dive deeper into understanding a particular issue, pain point or product set.

Level 4 (Gold Star) Incorporate an ethnographic study—basically, observing your customers and prospects in their natural environment, with the aim of identifying the otherwise hidden buying motivations and contexts in which customers may use a new product or service. This may be a bit more intensive than other market research methodologies, but it's especially helpful for companies engaged in complex business-to-business marketing and long sales cycles. To observe how customers interact with you in the digital world you could do a netnographic study, looking at how they behave in the digital world.

The Art of Interviewing

There are several books dedicated to explaining the art of good questioning—especially as it relates to the world of journalism, where a good story only emerges when the interviewer effectively probes the interviewee. One book in particular, *Interviewing Users: How to Uncover Compelling Insights* by Steve Portigal, provides practical advice on how to structure and conduct interviews that yield quality information and understanding at a deeper level.

We want to touch briefly on the topic here, as we believe this is a foundational skill that marketers need to develop in order to uncover customer insights in a way that will help set your organisation apart.

Be Curious All good interviewers have a curious mindset. This means they are open to learning and accepting new ideas and the possibility that things may be different from how they originally thought. Come from a place of genuine interest to understand how your customers perceive the world and seek to understand what their assumptions are.

Make Them Feel Comfortable You want to help your customers feel relaxed and 'at home' with you during the interview. Your goal should be to create a trusting environment so that they feel safe about opening up and sharing their story.

Ask Open-Ended Questions A good interview requires some prep work. Spend some time coming up with a list of appropriate, interesting and creative questions. Think about what you really want to know, then develop questions that help you dig deeper. Avoid questions that have a yes/no answer, as these will not provide you with the greater understanding that you are seeking. Here are some ideas to get you started.

- What are the biggest challenges you currently face?
- What are your top three initiatives/ priorities this year?
- What is the one thing you wish your vendors would do to make your job easier?
- What do you think we can do to improve as a company?
- What do you like best (or least) about the current solution? Why?
- Why did you choose to do business (or stop doing business) with our firm?
- What do you think about XYZ competitor?
- Do you have any advice on how we can be a better partner?
- Which tasks take you longer to complete than you'd like?
- How do you measure success?
- What does your ideal solution look like?

Actively Listen Most of us don't really listen to what's being said. Instead, we are too busy thinking about how we want to respond to the other person. Tune in and pay attention to what your customer is saying. Make it a habit to reflect back what you've heard, which ensures you don't misunderstand or misinterpret the other person's views and comments.

Final Thoughts: Staying Ahead

There is no doubt that understanding what matters most to your customers requires an ongoing effort. And, like forming any new habit, you have to be consistent if you want this to become part of your new routine. You may not have a full-time resource dedicated to gathering customer intelligence, which means it's everyone's job to seek out and share information across the organisation.

Luckily, there are ways to make it easier to collect information.

Leverage Online Resources

There are hundreds of speciality databases available to collect and capture data about your potential customers. One of the best resources is Hoovers, an online tool that provides validated information and analysis at company level as well as at industry level.

Talk to Customers Whenever You Can

This may seem obvious, and yet it is often the most overlooked method. Are you taking advantage of the events, seminars and tradeshows that your customers attend? For example, we've seen many marketers who are standing shoulder to shoulder with potential customers at an event or tradeshow, only to clam up or push some product literature in their prospect's face. This is a perfect opportunity to pay attention and let your prospect do the talking. Pick up on the language they use, who they view as your competition and what their biggest priorities are.

Ask Your Sales Team to Be Involved

Salespeople can be very protective of their customers, controlling what information the customer receives/hears about your company. But we have noticed that the most successful salespeople recognise that sales is a whole-company effort and will not ignore a request from their marketing team to get on the phone or meet their customers. In fact, they will welcome it, as it means they'll likely learn something they haven't thought to ask their customer.

Analyse Data from All Sources

There's no use in gathering data if you simply aren't doing anything with it. We've covered extensively the tools and methods you can use to gather data, but don't forget the purpose of all this data is to help you make informed decisions. Carve out time to regularly review internal reports and third-party information in order to identify trends, themes and patterns.

Implement a Process to Conduct Win-Loss Analysis

Does your company formally review every new or lost sale? Without conducting a win/loss analysis, you are left with mere speculation as to why the customer chose (or didn't choose) your solution. Our advice is to formalise the programme internally in order to get into the habit of collecting valuable customer data and form a long-term view when it is fresh in the minds of sales. Companies often get stuck in short-term thinking, and ultimately never gain a complete picture as to why their customers do business with them! For example, one firm we met with recently lost a big bid. When the Propositions Manager asked the sales team to get involved in a 'loss' discussion, they shrugged their shoulders and said 'On to the next one'.

Further Reading

Bandler, R., & Grinder, J. (1979). *Frogs into princes*. Moab: Real People Press.

Braun, V., & Clarke, V. (2006). *Using thematic analysis in psychology*. Qualitative Research in Psychology, *3*(2), 77–101.

Ham, S. H. (1992). *Environmental interpretation: A practical guide for people with big ideas and small budgets*. Golden: North American Press.

Ham, S. H., & Weller, B. (2004). Diffusion and adoption of thematic interpretation at an interpretive historic site. *UNSW Annals of Leisure Research, 7*(1), 1–1.

Levitt, T. (1960). Marketing myopia. *Harvard Business Review, 38*, 24–47.

Portigal, S. (2013). *Interviewing users: How to uncover compelling insights*. Brooklyn: Rosenfeld Media.

Webster, F. E. (2002b). *Market-driven management: How to define, develop, and deliver customer value* (2nd ed.). Hoboken: Wiley.

5

Aligning Products and Solutions to Themes: From Bombardment to Customer Value Conversations

In this chapter we will look at:

- How to array solutions, products and services under the themes you have selected
- Developing a framework for understanding where you may have gaps in your offers
- Providing a methodology for cross-selling and upselling products and solutions
- Seeing a path for finding gaps, developing solutions and partnerships
- Developing a 'golden thread' that aligns product marketing to proposition themes

Crucially, at the end of the chapter you will be in a position to stop bombarding your customers with random feature-led product launches. Instead, you will be set up to be able to have a value-based conversation with them about how you can help solve their business problems.

Why Is This Important?

We have already seen that as far as customers are concerned it's absolutely not all about the product, far from it. We can point to a number of surveys that bear this out. For example, we know that when Forrester asked Fortune 500 C suite executives involved in buying decisions why they chose a certain vendor

© The Author(s) 2017
S. Kelly et al., *Value-ology*,
DOI 10.1007/978-3-319-45626-3_5

only 16 % cited a vendor's products, services or capabilities to be the most important factor separating them from the pack. Executives overwhelmingly believed that vendors who understood their business problems and could prescribe solutions to them were the ones that won out. Despite this, only 27 % of C level executives found salespeople knowledgeable about their business.

We live in an era when business is most often lost to customer inertia, where customers are highly likely to do nothing if they are not convinced of the need to change. Jill Konrath observes in *Agile Selling* (2015) that buyers increasingly keep sellers out, because in their experience most are 'Product-pushing peddlers who don't bring any value to the decision making process, ask stupid questions, offer minimal insights and give boring presentations'.

We also know that increasingly customers are concerned about how they are sold to, not just what they are sold. Corporate Executive Board (CEB) research cited in *The Challenger Sale* (2011) showed that 53 % of customers said their loyalty was enhanced by sales reps—if they bring valuable help and insights. So if you bring insight into the sales process and show understanding of the customers' business issues you are providing them with differentiation in your approach.

We also saw in Chap. 2 that even organisations that rate themselves highly for value proposition development still run to product comparisons when asked what sets them apart. No wonder they have difficulty articulating how they differentiate themselves from competitors. We've pointed out the danger in starting at the top of our value stack at account-based marketing level without establishing proposition themes and failing to array products against them.

In this chapter we'll give you the tools that will help you have an ongoing conversation with customers about the issues that affect them, and how your products and services can solve these problems. This framework will allow you to introduce new products seamlessly by integrating them under the umbrella themes. This should signal the end of 'boring presentations' that portray your organisation as a bunch of product peddlers. It could be the beginning of a rich and fruitful path to sales and revenue growth based on customer conversations that add value to their business and yours.

Selecting Proposition Themes

We saw in Chap. 4 that there's no magic bullet for selecting proposition themes. The answer you get to should be underpinned by a deep level of understanding of the issues that affect your customer. You can only get this by committing a level of emotional, physical and financial resource into researching these issues. After you've performed your research you get to the proposition themes through a combination of 'thematic analysis' and right-brain creativity.

In the end what matters is that the themes:

- Resonate with customers
- Provide a platform for communication
- Support development of sector, segment and customer value propositions
- Provide a clear opportunity for your organisation because you understand the revenue and profitability upsides
- Create conversations that lead to the solutions you provide to help solve the customer problems

The main purpose of this chapter is to move you from a position where you have decided on the proposition themes to one where you have arrayed your solutions, products and services under these themes. This will allow you to have perpetual value theme conversations with your customers. If you have a lot of products, you can 'chunk up' into product categories or families to help you in the quest to stop bombarding the customer with 'product push' messages. Remember, 94 % of them said they would check out of your electronic building if you continued with product push! Before we go on to explain how to array your solutions under the themes we thought it might be helpful to provide a couple of models that may help with theme selection.

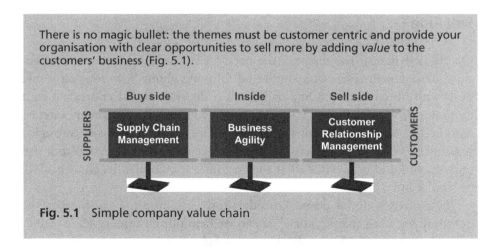

There is no magic bullet: the themes must be customer centric and provide your organisation with clear opportunities to sell more by adding *value* to the customers' business (Fig. 5.1).

Fig. 5.1 Simple company value chain

How Do Your Customers Create Value for Their Customers?

There are numerous models out-there that describe how organisations work to create value. Perhaps the most famous is Michael Porter's value chain, which was introduced in his iconic book *Competitive Advantage: Creating and Sustaining Superior Performance* (1985).

A value chain is a set of activities that a company performs to create value for its customers. The way these value chain activities are executed affect costs and profits and ultimately the way value is provided to customers.

Porter divided these activities into primary and support activities. Primary activities consist of inbound logistics, operations, outbound logistics, marketing, and sales and service. Support activities consist of procurement, HR management, technological development and infrastructure. These primary and support activities work together to help create a valuable product or service for customers.

We have only briefly introduced this here as a potential tool to help you create themes. We have always preferred to chunk up to provide a simpler view of an organisation value chain to help you with broader theme development. We would prefer to view this as a customer demand chain which starts from the relationship your organisation has with its customers. We acknowledge that a model such as Porter's value chain may help you with deeper customer understanding of your customers as you move towards the top of the value chain. For now, let's focus on how our simple model helps theme development.

Sell Side

On the sell side of the diagram the overarching issue is customer relationship management. Here you should be thinking about how your customer deals with his customers. On a daily basis it depends on the context of your customer. If your customer is a manufacturer how do its customers interact with it? Is it through account managers? Are regular orders placed through a website? How does the end customer make decisions about buying from this organisation and others like it? If the customer is a retailer, its concerns will be similar but different.

These matters are for deeper consideration further up the value stack. The question you need to ask yourself is can we help our customers achieve their sell-side objectives? Do we think we can help enough to develop a major proposition theme in this area?

After all, the different contextual concerns of the manufacturer or retailer roll up to overall objectives of customer acquisition, growth or retention. Depending on the circumstances there will be varying levels of concern about profitability and competitive threat.

If you decide to develop a proposition theme in this area it's likely to be around customer relationship management, customer growth or competitive advantage. In this internet age it may be around how you can help customers provide a secure service to their customers.

Inside

The inside of the organisation, in simple terms, is concerned with making sure it's agile enough to deal with what's coming at it from the sell side to drive innovation back into the buy side, or simply to deliver against customer requests. In this omni-channel environment this is becoming increasingly important as customers expect to be able to receive a 'tailored solution' at the point of interaction with a company website.

Underneath this heading the specific issues of the sector or customer could be about the customer experience, and there may be issues about how efficiently customer orders are being processed. There could be concerns around how the organisation learns from previous experience on the one hand to straightforward operating costs on the other.

If you decide to develop a proposition theme in this area it's likely to be about how you can help your customers be more agile, faster or more efficient.

Buy Side

The left-hand side of the model is all about how the organisation interacts with its supply chain providing a strong tie back to Porter's inbound logistics. Under this heading there could be issues relating to speed and quality of delivery, information transfer and costs of supply. There may also be concerns about supplier relationships. For the largest suppliers there may be issues around their providing innovation to help your organisation exploit new opportunities.

If you think you can help your customers improve their supply chain management you are likely to develop proposition themes that focus on supply chain efficiency, taking costs out of the supply chain. You may be able to support a theme that talks about improved availability or better overall supply chain management.

We would advocate taking more of a demand chain management (DCM) focus. This focuses on managing customer and supplier relationships aimed at delivering best customer value at least cost to the demand chain. If you believe that you can support organisations to improve their demand chain you are likely to develop proposition themes around speed, innovation and efficiency.

We have used this model to help organisations think about issues that affect their customers and to help them develop themes. We acknowledge there are other sources that can help you with inspiration. For example, in his article 'The triple A supply chain' (2004) Lee talks about how Alignment (shared incentives), Agility (ability to respond quickly to changes) and Adaptability (ability to adjust the design of the supply chain) can help organisations enhance the value they provide to customers. We have already introduced Jeff Thull's work in his book *The Prime Solution*, where he categorises eight typical business drivers in three big blocks around Financial Performance, Quality and Competitiveness. They provide useful pointers that can help with theme development.

We still run into sales people from organisations who have used our simple value chain model who talk about it fondly as something they can use to anchor customer value conversations. At the end of the chapter we have provided a simple template that helps you think about the issues customers face under our simple value chain model headings.

Aligning Themes and Products

Once you have identified what the key business issues are for your customers, you're in a position to choose proposition themes that relate to these key issues. You should now be ready to array your products, services and solutions under these theme headings to ensure you have continuous value conversations with your customers.

Let's start with an everyday business-to-customer (B2C) example that we should all be familiar with to explain the concept, before we dive into how we suggest applying this in a business-to-business (B2B) world. If you were setting up a restaurant you wouldn't say 'we sell food', then list all the products you sell. Strange how we see this approach so often in B2B. The Cheesecake Factory, which is renowned in the USA for having a broad menu, has a 'something for everyone' theme. This is their overarching foundational value proposition.

Let's say you've performed customer, market and competitor research and found an opportunity to provide healthy, nutritious and locally sourced organic food. You decide that 'healthy' and 'nutritious' are the main themes that will resonate with your customers. In the approach we're advocating we suggest that before you get to the product menu card you array what it is you offer under these two themes. Of course you can highlight how individual 'signature' products support these proposition themes. For example, Cracker Barrel Old Country Stores in the USA has an overall proposition about making 'Healthy homestyle cooking made from quality ingredients cooked from scratch'. It uses individual recipes to help support this claim, which is linked to the overall value themes. This means they're always talking to the customer about their major themes. The products are described as 'solutions' that fit underneath these themes.

Exercise 5.1 Let's assume you're going to open this new healthy and nutritious dining experience. Think about how you could develop a set of 'offers' underneath these two themes of health and nutrition.

From Bombardment to Value Relevance

So, let's return to our B2B world. The very first time we implemented this approach we had the challenge of helping a company find a more effective way of communicating with customers than bombarding them with over 1000 different products. In order to ensure anonymity we'll label the product families we arrived at alphabetically.

Using our simple value chain model the company took the view that there was more mileage in developing themes on the sell side and inside of the organisations it was trying to develop business with. This led to more potential opportunities to provide value to customers, which in turn would drive revenue and profit growth. The company also took the view that going for two themes would mean that it would only need to run two overarching 'foundational' campaigns through the year, one per theme. The two themes selected were 'Agility' and 'Customer Relationship'.

The hundreds of products in the company portfolio were placed into nine product families or categories. We don't take it as a given that you'll have gone to the trouble of creating these product families, so there may be work to be done here too. If your organisation has fewer products then this may not be a concern. You should still array your individual products against the themes you've chosen.

You can see that some of the product categories span both themes. This is where some B2B marketers sometimes get blocked. 'Well, you could put all of your products under both categories' is an objection we've heard more than once. Well, guess what, that's the point! In B2C marketing there isn't a problem with this concept. Coca-Cola has used happiness as a theme for a good number of years. Many other companies have also emulated this approach, using happiness as a platform to promote their different products. Probably this is because for human beings happiness trumps everything; it's something we all aspire to, so it's a great proposition theme to appeal to.

We can also see from the example that this objection is not entirely true. If we look at Fig. 5.2, we can see that Product Family H would impact on the CRM theme while Product Family G only applies to Agility. Going back to our restaurant example, I'm sure you could categorise some things as more healthy than nutritious and vice versa. Four of the product families in our B2B example span fully across both themes. What's great about this is that it makes you stop talking about the features of the products and forces you to think about how, for example, 'Product Family I' helps organisations become more agile or can help them connect to their customers more effectively. The other thing is that you have a perpetual platform to have value conversations about some of your core products—to move the discussion away from features and price.

You will see in Chaps. 6 and 7 how this pulls through into message and campaign development.

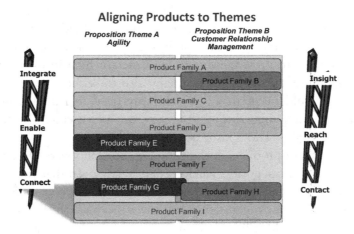

Fig. 5.2 Theme and product alignment canvas – aligning products to themes

Proposition Ladders

The reason we advocate developing proposition ladders is to take your customers on an upward journey with you. This journey should lead them to a point of excellence related to the theme. At the top of the ladder they will be truly agile, or demonstrating customer insight.

You can see in Fig. 5.3 that we developed a proposition ladder for each theme. The product families are aligned to the rung of the ladder that best fits the benefits they can bring to the customer. For example, Product Family I helps customers 'connect' to agility and helps them contact customers.

In Fig. 5.3 we can see the CRM proposition ladder blown out to show the benefits that customers can get as they travel up the rungs. On the bottom rung it's all about customer contact. For this company it moved the customer conversations away from product push towards being about enhancing customer contact and customer experience. Climbing to the middle of the ladder moves the conversation towards how new customers can be reached. This time the conversation shifts away from price towards helping open up new channels and markets. At the top of the ladder you're providing customer insight solutions that help organisations think about how they gather and analyse customer data to provide insight into new trends and opportunities. A distant walk away from a price discussion.

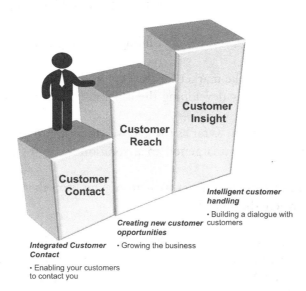

Fig. 5.3 Developing a proposition ladder that takes a customer on an upward journey

Gaps and Partnerships

Where we have helped organisations with this 'all-in' approach to value proposition development it has provided a great framework for identifying gaps, building solutions and pointing the way towards the need to partner.

By focusing on what the customer is trying to achieve inside each proposition theme and working this through, you'll develop a good understanding of what it takes to be truly agile or customer centred, depending on the themes you've selected. The ladders give us a view to the journey from rung 1 to top rung agility, or whatever theme you've chosen.

When you start to array your products, services and solutions onto the ladder it'll soon become apparent that there are gaps. In the above example it forced the company to consider if its product portfolio really helped customers develop customer insight. Did it have an offer in Product Family G that helped customers 'enable' business agility? If at this point you believe you have a gap then you're back to Strategic Marketing 101 and need to answer the next question: fill the gap or not?

Fill the Gap or Not?

If there is a gap, whether and how to fill it becomes a key question for the business. Some questions that you need to ask yourself at this point are:

- Is the gap big enough to be worth filling? How big is the potential profit pool?
- How competitive is the market for the gap product?
- Can we fill the gap by developing the capability ourselves or by buying it in?
- Does our brand stretch as far as the gap we are trying to fill?
- Is the gap product fundamental to a solution we want to offer to the customer?
- Would it make sense to partner with an organisation that is more credible in the area where the gap is?

Of course you've 'done the math' through your research to understand how big the theme market is. In this example you'll know what the overall size of the Agility or CRM market is. Depending on how granular your work is, you may already know how big the potential market is for the gaps you've identified. If not, you'll need to do some more groundwork to help answer the Strategic Marketing 101 questions relating to potential size, profit and competitiveness of the gap market. Hopefully you can see that this is a great way to think about who you may need to partner with. If you decide that the gap is worth filling and that it's better to fill by partnering, the next decision is whom to partner with.

Developing Solutions

The proposition ladder approach can also help you decide which solutions you wish to develop. 'Solution' is a word we've used a number of times already, so it's probably worth providing a definition to avoid any doubt. It's certainly a word we see being used interchangeably with value proposition inside organisations, which can be a source of unnecessary confusion.

The Oxford English Dictionary definition for solution is:

A means of solving a problem or dealing with a difficult situation.

The example sentence they provide to illustrate the definition is:

There are no easy solutions to financial and marital problems.

Building on the financial problems element. If you were providing a counselling service you might have an overall proposition about helping individuals feel more in control of their finances. The solution that you offer might include a number of counselling sessions, some self-help tools and maybe an audit and analysis of spending. The overall solution is made up of the services you're proposing to help overcome the finance problem. We acknowledge that an individual product, let's say counselling sessions, may solve the financial problem in its own right.

So, the control proposition is the promise of helping clients gaining control of their finance problems. The solution, as we would define it, is:

The collection of products and services that provide the customer the means of solving a problem. The solution is the means of delivering the value proposition.

If we go back to our example illustrated in Fig. 5.3, we can see that we have an overall agility proposition. We can start to develop overall agility solutions, though it makes more sense to break these down in line with the ladder rungs. So at the bottom of the agility ladder we have a connect proposition, under which we can develop connectivity solutions. This helps elevate customer conversations away from individual products towards solutions that deliver customer value. Hopefully you can see that this can solve the typical problem that many organisations have in selling beyond the first product.

Grouping individual products into an overall solution is what we come to now, using another adapted example from a customer project for a mobile company.

Building a Solution

This adapted example is taken from a period of recession in a country served by a mobile phone company. The company was interested in the key issues serving small businesses in this context. The problems the mobile phone company was facing were about losing small and medium-sized enterprise (SME) business to rival operators, declining margins driven by price discussions and having a high percentage of single product customers.

Working with the client, we found that businesses like this had typically survived the start-up phase and begun to expand. At this stage it was not uncommon for the company leader to feel that he was losing control—of his customers, people, costs and his work/life balance.

Now he has more customers, competitors, people and costs, and less time. He may feel that he needs to regain control from a financial, managerial, emotional and whole life perspective.

In the prevailing economic climate, controlling costs and people is fundamental to business survival. A business's ability to raise money will become harder; margins are becoming squeezed as the result of rising costs and tightening market conditions. There may be a slowdown in sales and competition will also increase as companies vie for sales.

From our research we recommended that the mobile company should lead with a control proposition to small businesses:

You (the SME leader) will feel in control of your business by….

Working with individual customers would facilitate developing control value propositions for them consistent with their business:

Bloggs and co. can gain control of their business, resulting in a 10 % reduction in operating costs by….

So, the *by…* becomes the solution that provides the means to deliver against the value proposition. Here we worked with the organisation to put together its piece part products into a solution to deliver against the control proposition (Fig. 5.4).

Before jumping to this, we broke down the individual challenges faced by SMEs using the framework in Fig. 5.5. For brevity we've not listed all the challenges we identified; what's important here are the headings. This gave an indication of the type of benefits the SME was looking to see delivered by the mobile phone company.

Challenges	Requirements	Barriers to resolution	Primary Needs
Protect margins and cash flow	Ability to manage costs without impacting the business' ability to grow; Minimise impact on business / survive economic downturns	Multiple cost streams out of control	Known controlled costs
Maximise sales in increasingly competitive market	Remain cost /price competitive in the market.	Lack of IT awareness and understanding around the key devices and tools to use	Pro-active account management

Fig. 5.4 Elements of control proposition

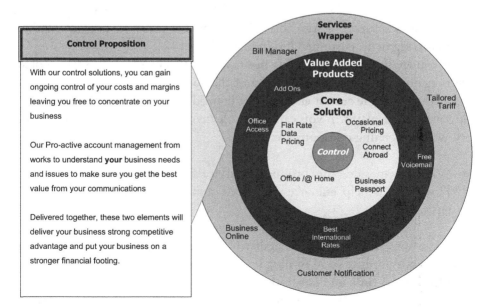

Fig. 5.5 The solution play

We used the value onion approach that we first introduced in Chap. 1. You can see that it begins with the core solution and builds out through value added services to a service wrapper. This has the added effect of building on post-sale customer service in the solution. Hopefully you can see that this again lifts the conversation away from price towards customer value, away from individual products towards solutions. There is a simple template at the end of this chapter that should help you do this for your own organisation.

The Golden Thread

Hopefully you can see that this approach gives you a 'golden thread' from proposition themes down to the marketing of individual products and services. Building on the value stack model we presented in Chap. 2, we develop proposition themes which can be used to broadcast to all our customers based on issues our research tells us are important to them. We further refine these at industry sector or segment level, develop greater resonance at customer level and create truly resonating value propositions for individuals in the customer organisation.

We recommend that as you move up our value stack model you review and refine the theme/product alignment canvas. For example, is managed desktop important to financial services customers? How vital is mobile voice and data to the manufacturing sector? This will allow you to prioritise product families at sector, segment, customer and individual level.

If you are in a customer-facing business unit this method gives you protection against random product launches that boast meaningless features that create noise for the customer. If you are in product marketing, you have a rolling marketing platform you can jump on that provides far greater coverage. Now your opening questions are:

• Which themes does my product or service sit under?
• How does it help enhance the theme and what are the benefits to the customer?

So in our earlier example, if agility is the lead campaign theme when you launch your product you just plug into all the activity in the campaign. There is a huge cost, time and frustration saving here as it takes away the need to have a campaign to launch or promote every single product individually. We have provided a simple template at the end of the chapter to help you consider these questions.

The golden thread is provided by the themes, and pulls through as far as individual products. This gives the customer a cohesive view of your organisation that is focused on issues they face that can be resolved by you. They will thank you for taking away the product blah, blah and boring presentations that are all about you. In our experience the thanks comes in the form of your revenue growth.

In Chap. 6 we discuss how to develop messaging to support this approach.

Further Reading

Konrath, J. (2015). *Agile selling: Get up to speed quickly in today's ever-changing sales world*. New York: Portfolio.

Lee, H.L. (2004). The triple a supply chain. *Harvard Business Review, 82*(10), 1–12.

Thull, J. (2016). *The prime solution: Close the value gap, increase margins, and win the complex sale*. Amazon Digital Services.

6

Your Buyer's Journey: Developing a Consistent Message

In this chapter we will look at:

- A framework to understand how your buyers make decisions about your product or service
- How to determine the different types of content you need to create in order to keep your buyer moving along their journey
- How to stop producing content that your sales team and customers don't need
- What to do to address organisations with multiple decision makers

By now, we have established that before you even think about creating marketing or sales content, you need to conduct research to understand what it is that your customers value most, and then select themes that appropriately position your solution in the right context.

Now we will look at how to bring your value proposition and customer themes into consistent and relevant content.

If you only take away one thing from this chapter, let it be this: *relevance is king*. And in this omni-channel world where potential customers interact with your brand through multiple touchpoints, *consistency is queen*. Look at any successful business and you will see that their results and growth were not an accident: they came from their ability to focus on a handful of closely connected initiatives and consistently follow-through. When it comes to content creation, and the delivery of your message to the marketplace, your approach should be no different. How you tell your story to a prospect through all of

© The Author(s) 2017
S. Kelly et al., *Value-ology*,
DOI 10.1007/978-3-319-45626-3_6

your customer touchpoints could be the difference between winning and losing a sale.

Your prospect is a moving target and interacts with your brand in a variety of ways—through your website, e-newsletter, social media, meetings with the sales team, customer service phone calls and more. And they likely aren't the only one in the organisation that you have to convince. But how do you make sure you're delivering a consistent story across all of these channels? To multiple decision-makers? Before we dive in, let's look at a quick example of how content marketing can make an impact.

From Tyre Company to Fine Dining Reviewer

Content marketing is not new. In fact, one of the best examples of content marketing is the *Michelin Guide*. In 1900, at a time when car ownership was very low in France, tyre manufacturers André and Edouard Michelin decided to publish a guide to help promote the idea that vehicle owners should get out and use their cars to travel long distances. The forward-thinking brothers figured that the more people drove, the quicker they would need to replace their tyres. The original guide included local maps, instructions on how to repair a tyre and the location of nearby mechanics, hotels, restaurants and petrol stations. The guides were passed out to drivers with every new car purchase. As their tyre company grew throughout Europe, they launched country-specific versions of the *Michelin Guide*, which they started to charge for in 1920. In 1926, the guide expanded to include fine dining, and today the Michelin star rating system is recognised as the gold standard for restaurants in twenty-four countries.

So how does a tyre company become the world's most famous and prestigious fine dining reviewer? Quite simply, it all started because they understood that their customers valued quality and a luxurious lifestyle that included travelling and fine dining. They also understood that in order to sell more tyres, they needed to appeal to vehicle owners and offer unique value that no other tyre company was offering. And so the *Michelin Guide* was born!

Today's Challenge

Marketing has seen rapid change and development over the past fifty years. In 1950, without a lot of competing entertainment options, families would sit around their radio or TV and flip between the few programmes available until they found something they wanted to listen to or watch. In the USA, this presented a huge opportunity for advertisers, as they could all but guarantee to reach millions of viewers during a single programme. Marketing messages were classified as 'push' messages, as companies sought to buy the airwaves and push whatever marketing message they wanted to as many people as they could—this was mostly describing their product and saying how great it was. On the business-to-business (B2B) side, the salesperson used to control the information their prospective customer would receive, and this was limited to in-person or phone interactions.

Since the arrival of the internet, and more video, audio, text and web content than we can handle, all this has changed. Now your potential customer is in the driver's seat, deciding which channels to tune into, whether to watch commercials or fast forward through them, click on or ignore your website advertisement or enter his/her email address to download your further information. With the click of a button, customers can call/text/chat/tweet/etc. to share their experiences of your company. And instead of waiting for a salesperson or customer service rep to come to them, they turn to the internet to find answers to their questions online.

Organisations continue to spend billions of dollars to create their own branded content. But, only 30 % of these organisations are finding their content effective (CMI 2016). Further, up to 70 % of the content produced by marketers is never used by the sales team (Sirius Decisions). So why isn't everyone experiencing the massive success that content marketing promises to deliver?

While there is a lot of advice about *what* to create, we have found that most organisations are focusing on the quantity of content they are producing instead of the quality. Marketers are under pressure to fuel the content engine—whether it's blog posts, videos or social media posts. Instead of allocating their resources to producing high-quality and impactful content, companies seem to be using every tactic available while struggling to determine how effective each approach really is. A case in point. When we asked a senior marketer which content she'd found to be the most effective at advancing the sale, she said, 'You'd better ask the sales guys.'

Truly effective content must strike the right balance of education and entertainment and *always* relate back to what the target audience cares about most. In other words, the content has to be relevant to your target audience and help its members along their decision journey. Otherwise there's no point in creating it.

In the last chapter we showed you how to identify themes that will resonate with your customers. Now we turn our attention to creating a consistent and purposeful set of messaging and content.

'Everyone is not your customer': Seth Godin

Who Is Your Target Buyer?

Before you can develop a value proposition or any content that resonates with your prospective customer, you have to do the work to truly understand who they are, what they value and how they make decisions.

The best tool to help you gain this level of understanding and confidence is the buyer persona (Fig. 6.1a, b). If you're not familiar with buyer personas,

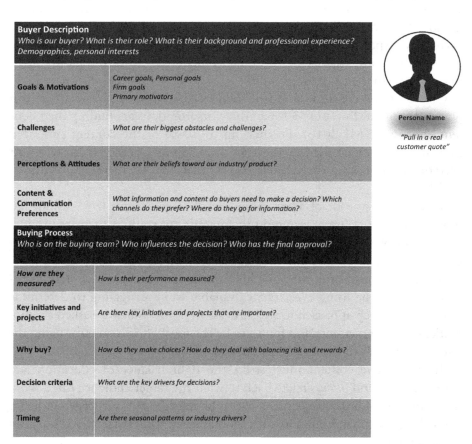

Fig. 6.1   Buyer persona framework: (**a**) Buyer overview. (**b**) Buyer process

Tony Zambito, founder of and leading authority on buyer personas, describes them as:

> Research-based archetypal (modeled) representations of who buyers are, what they are trying to accomplish, what goals drive their behavior, how they think, how they buy, why they make buying decisions, where they buy as well as when buyers decide to buy.

They are essentially a generalised, fictitious representation of your prospective buyer, based on real customer information. They help you understand what your customers are thinking, and what they are motivated and challenged by as they evaluate their purchases.

Taking the time to create personas ultimately ensures that you:

- Get the best return for your marketing and sales efforts
- Create stronger messaging and deeper connection with your buyers
- Provide solutions that seem tailor-made for your audience. Buyers are 48 % more likely to consider solution providers that tailor marketing content to address their concerns (ITSMA)
- Develop personalised content. For example, instead of sending the same lead nurturing emails to everyone in your database, you can segment by buyer persona and tailor your messaging according to what you know about those different personas
- Address specific people, problems and beliefs

Companies that successfully develop and deploy buyer personas internally have seen some worthwhile results:

- Email open rates double and click-through rates are five times better (Single Grain)
- Personalised emails drove eighteen times more revenue than broadcast emails
- Websites became —two to five times more effective and easier to use (HubSpot)
- 124 % increase in sales leads and 97 % increase in online leads (Skytap case study)
- 72 % reduction in lead conversion time (Thompson Reuter case study)

Surprisingly, only 44 % of B2B marketers are using buyer personas, and 85 % aren't using them effectively.[1] A major roadblock in the way of imple-

---

[1] © ITSMA Online Survey: *Increasing Relevance with Buyer Personas and B2I Marketing*, March 2014.

menting buyer personas is that many marketers aren't doing enough qualitative research on their buyers. In Tony Zambito's State Of Buyer Personas Study (2016), only 25 % of 124 marketing executives surveyed relied on the needed in-depth qualitative research.[2] Instead, firms are sourcing their customer intelligence from their sales teams, which may offer some insight, but not the complete view of their buyers. Essentially these are just empty shells with no substance!

On the flipside, many marketers are spending inordinate amounts of time figuring out too many unnecessary details that are, frankly, useless in complex B2B sales situations. For example, when developing a buyer persona for your B2B solution, does the knowledge that your buyer loves chocolate chip ice-cream apply? Of course it doesn't. The main problem here is a basic lack of understanding of what type of information to process and what to leave out.

As one senior marketer told us, it's difficult to create and implement personas with consistency and discipline throughout the organisation. It requires constant reminding to content creators, sales personnel and product managers to reference and make decisions based on the personas. In Chap. 9, we discuss ways in which the marketing and sales team can better align around the customer, and personas can be an impactful way in which to start to bridge that gap.

Our buyer persona framework is divided into two sections. Section 1 (Fig. 6.1a) focuses on understanding who your buyer is as a person. This covers areas such as:

• Background information
• Previous experience
• Their role
• Personal interests
• Goals and motivations
• Challenges they are facing
• Their perceptions toward your industry/firm
• Their communication preferences

Section 2 (Fig. 6.1b) focuses more on the purchasing process, and includes:

• Understanding their role in the purchase
• How they will be measured

---

[2] Zambito, T. (2016) *State of Buyer Personas Study* [Online] Available at: http://tonyzambito.com/state-buyer-personas-2016-results-strong-correlation-effectiveness-goals/.

- What key initiatives and projects they are working on
- The decision criteria and how they make a decision
- Timing

In our experience, where companies get tripped up is in focusing on Section 1—the 'buyer overview'—only, and fail to understand the buyer's role, criteria and motivations related to the purchasing process. While it can be fun to speculate on what sports your fictitious customers play, the real purpose of developing personas is to gain the deep customer understanding that we've been referring to throughout the book.

Here are some tips that will help make your buyer personas more successful:

- *Explain to your organisation why you are developing personas.* Having a deep customer understanding impacts more than just the marketing department. For example, the HR (human resources) department is responsible for hiring the employees who will ultimately deliver on the customer value proposition. But how can HR be sure to find the right type of people if they don't understand what your customers expect from your organisation?
- *Update them.* After you've done the work to create personas, confirm their authenticity and keep them up to date. Remember, there will always be nuances (such as job titles/personal interests), but you are looking for broad generalisations. As new industry or third-party data becomes available, look to validate how this impacts your customers.
- *Share with the rest of the organisation.* The entire organisation, not just customer-facing personnel, should understand who your firm's ideal customer is. Further, train each department on how they should be using this information to make decisions: from customer communications and new product development to billing preferences, content creation and sales meetings.

The Buying Experience

We'd like to think that the buying process is linear, meaning that your buyer moves neatly from one stage to the next. But this isn't exactly the case. Your buyer interacts with your company in a dynamic way, especially if you have multiple products and services to offer. A customer may be at the end of the process for one problem, while not yet aware of another problem. In addition, if a buyer is unsatisfied with the information available as s/he learns more about their problem, s/he may become stuck at a particular stage, or even move backwards until gaining a solid grasp on the issue.

It is important to point out that both marketing and sales have a role in understanding customers and their journeys. Marketing will utilise this information to produce more compelling and relevant content that helps to bring customers through the door, while sales will use this information to aid their customers along the journey toward a solution.

There are numerous frameworks out there to describe the buying process. Our model (Fig. 6.2) assumes your buyer goes through five major stages as s/he decides to work with you.

1. Awareness

First, your buyer has to become aware of a problem that exists in his/her world. Generally something has to happen for the buyer to move from 'unaware' to 'aware'. This could be something small, such as a colleague pointing out a problem, or it could be something large, such as complete failure of the current solution. The buyer is seeking to learn more about the problem and to ultimately determine whether or not the problem is big enough to fix.

For example, let's say your customer is an IT (information technology) director responsible for deciding which laptops to deploy to his organisation. He starts to get complaints from employees about the unstable operating system and poor battery life of the current brand of laptops. At the same time, there are numerous laptops that are old and need replacing. So now he needs to decide

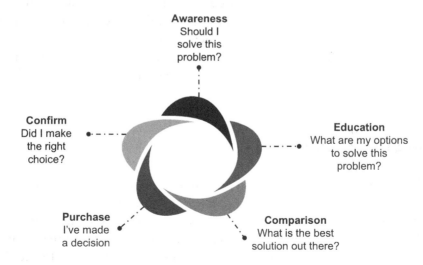

Fig. 6.2 The buyer's journey

whether or not to continue to deploy the same brand/model of laptops, or seek an alternative solution.

2. Education

   Once your buyer becomes aware of his/her problem and has made the decision to solve it, s/he starts to seek more information about *how* to solve it, using generic web search terms, talking to peers and tapping into social networks, to see if anyone has encountered a similar situation. The buyer starts to develop a list of criteria based upon research and determines the most important factors of a solution.

   Carrying on our example, the IT director may talk to his peers or look at review boards to see if others are having the same type of problems with this particular brand of laptop. If he's had a positive experience with the laptop company, he may call directly and see what the company recommends. Perhaps he will seek input from other organisations regarding the brand of laptops they use and how happy they are with the support they receive. In addition, he may need to bring in other decision-makers to make sure everyone understands the problem and is weighing all the options.

3. Comparison

   Once the buyer has a basic idea of what he/she needs, s/he starts looking for specific vendors/products/services to fix the problem. Educated on the features/benefits, s/he compares your pricing with that of your competitors. Your buyer may also ask to talk to some of your other customers to see what their experience has been like, also looking at the option of continuing with business as usual (maintaining the status quo). If the buying process seems too cumbersome, expensive and overwhelming, a buyer might make the decision to wait it out.

   By now the IT director has a good idea of what he needs and the laptop brands that can meet his criteria. He has done all of this research up to this point on his own, without involving the vendor's sales team. He finally calls to talk to a sales rep in order to learn the pricing, support and billing options. (As we've pointed out in earlier chapters, the buyer is about 60 % through his decision-making process at this point.) He then compares all this information with his current solution and presents a compelling recommendation to his manager (and others involved in the decision) about switching to a new brand of laptops.

4. Purchase

   The purchase phase is generally short. Your prospect may request a trial of your product or service instead of the full-blown solution, wanting to make sure the right choice is being made. At the end of this stage, your buyer makes a decision to go with your solution or a competitor.

Despite the learning curve involved in deploying and supporting a different brand of laptops, the IT director and his manager make a decision to switch. Their procurement team gets involved to negotiate the details of the contract with the new vendor.

5. Confirm

This is a critical moment for your buyer. Immediately following his/her decision, s/he looks for confirmation that the right decision has been made. The buyer will begin to evaluate whether or not the full benefits your solution promised to deliver are being received. Depending on how quickly these benefits, buyer's remorse may set in. On the other hand, if the onboarding experience is pleasant and pain-free, the buyer may start to refer your solution to friends and peers.

So far the experience has been satisfying for the IT director. He seamlessly replaced the older laptops with the new equipment. As he was configuring the new laptops he ran into some problems, which were easily resolved by the vendor's customer service team. In addition, the vendor provided him with a 'Getting started' guide to pass along to the users, helping them to become proficient as quickly as possible.

Exercise Now it's your turn. Using this framework, document how a prospective buyer goes through his/her journey to decide whether or not to buy from your organisation. Identify the questions your buyer asks along the way to determine how/when to move forward through the journey. Remember that buyers may jump back and forth between the stages if they don't feel they've found the right information or salesperson to help them along. This framework can be used for all of the products/ services that you offer.

Building Customer Touchpoints

After you've outlined your buyer's journey, it's time to take stock of the content your organisation has already created or will need to create.

Before we jump to the types of content to consider, however, we want to point out a few guiding principles.

1—Don't Contribute to the Noise
According to a report from IBM, nearly 15 petabytes of data are created every day—eight times more than the information in all libraries in the USA.

What this means for your customers is lots and lots of noise! We urge you not to contribute to the content explosion with sub-par, irrelevant content. A good rule of thumb is to start by asking your sales team what will help move the needle most. Ask them where they're getting stuck with customers during their buying journey. Analyse results from other pieces of content you've created (for example, on your website or on social media) to determine what works. Let this dictate where to focus your efforts, rather than chasing the next new marketing tactic.

2—Stop and Think

Do not just start executing tactics. Before you create any new piece of content, begin with the end in mind. You should be able to answer the following questions:

- Why do we need it?
- Is it relevant to the customer?
- Is this consistent with our overall brand message?
- How will it be distributed?
- Does it help advance the sale?
- Will our sales team use it?
- Which 'buying stage' does this content align with?

3—Consistency Matters

Lastly, and most importantly, remember that marketing requires a consistent drumbeat to steadily build up your firm's awareness and credibility. For example, look at Apple and the consistent delivery of the 'simplicity' message. This 'golden thread' is present in every part of the customer experience—from the company website, to retail stores, to product design.

Everything—and we mean everything—about your message needs to look, feel and sound consistent across channels. In addition, your message needs to be frequently shared in order to stick. Advertising gurus have long claimed that a prospect must be exposed to your message seven times before they can recall it. And, according to the Marketing Donut, 80 % of sales require five follow-ups.

We call this term 'frelevancy', meaning frequent relevancy. For example, If you had a highly relevant message, but shared it only once, nobody would see it. On the other hand, if you had an irrelevant message and spent millions of dollars broadcasting it, nobody would care. Further, you certainly don't want forty-five different salespeople sharing forty-five different messages about your company to your customers.

Now, with those principles in mind, it's on to the fun part: content creation! It's important to point out that it's not necessary to create all this content. Identify where you have gaps or where buyers might be getting stuck, and focus your resources to help them move more quickly through the decision process. For example, we hear from a lot of salespeople that the content gap tends to be in the later stages of the process—when case studies, references and other proof points are needed to help the customer make a decision. If left unattended, your sales team will likely just create this content on their own (which goes against your goal of one consistent message in the market), or worse, lose the sale because they don't have anything to share.

Fig. 6.3 provides a matrix that you can reference when thinking about what to create. You'll notice that we've aligned these tactics to the buying journey. And while there's certainly no single way to develop content, this framework will help you begin to think about focusing your internal resources into the areas that matter most for your customers.

Exercise It's time to see how well your company communicates a consistent message. Assess if every aspect of your brand's presence looks and feels consistent across every channel. Be sure to look at your website copy, blog posts, white papers, press

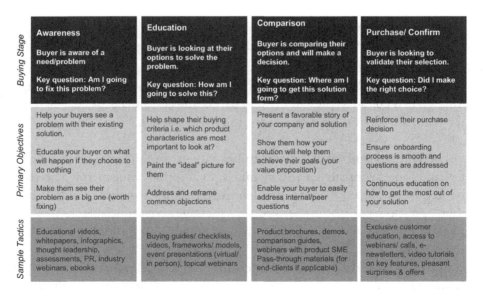

	Awareness	Education	Comparison	Purchase/ Confirm
Buying Stage	Buyer is aware of a need/problem Key question: Am I going to fix this problem?	Buyer is looking at their options to solve the problem. Key question: How am I going to solve this?	Buyer is comparing their options and will make a decision. Key question: Where am I going to get this solution form?	Buyer is looking to validate their selection. Key question: Did I make the right choice?
Primary Objectives	Help your buyers see a problem with their existing solution. Educate your buyer on what will happen if they choose to do nothing Make them see their problem as a big one (worth fixing)	Help shape their buying criteria i.e. which product characteristics are most important to look at? Paint the "ideal" picture for them Address and reframe common objections	Present a favorable story of your company and solution Show them how your solution will help them achieve their goals (your value proposition) Enable your buyer to easily address internal/peer questions	Reinforce their purchase decision Ensure onboarding process is smooth and questions are addressed Continuous education on how to get the most out of your solution
Sample Tactics	Educational videos, whitepapers, infographics, thought leadership, assessments, PR, industry webinars, ebooks	Buying guides/ checklists, videos, frameworks/ models, event presentations (virtual/ in person), topical webinars	Product brochures, demos, comparison guides, webinars with product SME Pass-through materials (for end-clients if applicable)	Exclusive customer education, access to webinars/ calls, e-newsletters, video tutorials on key features, pleasant surprises & offers

Fig. 6.3 Content mapping

releases, case studies, social media posts, sales presentations, product brochures, email signatures, requests for proposals and any other communication that your customer may see. Rate your communications on a three-point scale: (1) not consistent, (2) somewhat consistent, (3) very consistent. Once you've taken stock of your current situation, you'll know where your organisation needs to focus in order to clean up and deliver a uniform message.

Remember that creating high-quality, effective content takes time and you can't expect overnight success. Stick with it and be patient! As long as you're focusing on your customer, you *will* see results.

Now that you have a grasp on how to build value-orientated communications, in Chap. 7 we'll look at how to implement and operationalise this approach through integrated marketing campaigns.

Further Reading

Content Marketing Institute, Marketing Profs. *2016 Benchmarks, Budgets, and Trends—North America.*

Davis, K. (2011). *Slow down sell faster!* New York: American Management Association.

Zambito, T. (2016). *A guide to buyer persona development.*

Part 3

Mobilising Value-ology in Your Organisation

7

Developing Coherent Campaigns

Now that you have the fundamentals, in this chapter we will explore how to bring your value proposition to life through a series of collective marketing activities.

We will look at:

- The definition of a marketing campaign
- How to develop and structure your marketing campaigns using the central themes you identified in Chap. 5
- A framework outlining how to execute a successful campaign
- How to get your team on board to execute a solid campaign

Let's begin with a story.

Jane, a marketing leader at a well-known financial services company, had spent several weeks planning and working with her advertising agency—a reputable firm based in NYC, to develop a big marketing campaign. They were hoping to take advantage of a market downturn to promote some of her firm's products that perform particularly well during this type of market.

Jane spent hours poring through industry reports, mulling over competitor sites and even talking to a couple of sales reps in order to come up with the campaign message. She developed a marketing plan after sitting down with her team, and they outlined goals for the campaign, such as increased website visits, time on site, number of email subscribers, number of webinar attendees. She thought she had all of the right pieces lined up: a well-defined

© The Author(s) 2017
S. Kelly et al., *Value-ology*,
DOI 10.1007/978-3-319-45626-3_7

target audience, a catchy campaign tagline, compelling creative and content, an integrated direct marketing and media plan.

They were moving fast, so when the campaign was nearly ready to launch, Jane called a brief internal meeting and explained the campaign details to the sales team. Their response was lacklustre. They wondered why this campaign would be any different to previous marketing initiatives. They didn't see why their clients would be interested in a 'clever' webinar or find the 'catchy' collateral that the advertising firm created very useful. And while they thought the content *looked* great, it lacked substance and depth.

Despite the lukewarm internal response, the marketing team was ready to get the campaign out into the market. After all, they'd already invested significant time, energy and resources into the development of various marketing tactics. Over the next month, Jane and her team spent hundreds of thousands of dollars to generate a splash in the market. They used online advertising, sponsored email blasts and webinars. They tried to generate leads with the new value-added marketing content they had produced.

After forty-five days, the team had received only a handful of qualified leads. Their media budget was rapidly depleting, and they knew they couldn't continue to generate demand without paying for it. So Jane decided to pull the plug on the campaign. It just wasn't generating the results they had anticipated. In addition, the sales team wasn't engaged or interested, and her firm had moved on to other priorities as the market landscape shifted.

This is an all too familiar scenario happening in organisations across every industry. So what went wrong? Could something have been done to prevent wasting so many marketing dollars and resources? Or was this marketing campaign doomed from the beginning?

Exercise 1: What do you think went wrong with Jane's approach? Write down your thoughts, then let's compare them with ours!

The takeaways:

Campaigns must have a clear goal. It was unclear what Jane's marketing campaign was trying to achieve and how it fitted into the big picture for her firm. While she did set smaller, more tactical objectives, such as increased website visitors and webinar registrations, these goals did not set the overall vision for the campaign. In our view, this campaign was much more of a standalone initiative, as it wasn't being executed under a relevant customer theme.

Where was the buy-in? One of Jane's biggest mistakes, and ultimately what led to her failed campaign, is that she didn't spend the time to get buy-in from the sales organisation *before* developing her campaign. She created the marketing story and content in a bubble with her advertising agency.

Rather than checking in with the sales leaders, Jane was moving too fast and waited until the end to show them what the marketing department had come up with. Considering the important role sales plays in carrying the message forward to the customer, this was a huge miss. We cover the need to get sales buy in in some depth in Chap. 9.

It starts with the customer. By now, I'm sure you're picking up on the trend that your initiatives will only be as good as your customer understanding. While Jane did some quick market research, she didn't take the time to talk to customers directly to determine how big their pain points were; nor did she spend enough time with the sales team to understand customer feedback. As a result, the marketing content they developed lacked substance, insight and depth. There was no umbrella theme under which to talk about relevant customer benefits.

Are Marketing Campaigns Dead?

In 2014, Forrester Research declared the traditional marketing campaign 'dead' in favour of contextual marketing (Parrish 2014). Contextual marketing is essentially delivering real-time, personalised, interactive communications to individual buyers using data and insights to help them along their buying journey. Contextual marketing is seeing a rise because nearly 50 % of consumers don't trust digital ads, 38 % don't trust emails and 36 % don't trust information in branded apps. Thanks to the internet, today's buyers expect to find information about your product or service when and where they need it. They expect your content to genuinely help educate them about their situation and help them make a decision. They definitely do not want a generic sales pitch or a bombardment of marketing messages in their inbox.

We would argue that while *traditional* one-way marketing campaigns are no longer impactful, the very concept of a marketing campaign is still very much alive. First, unless your firm has unlimited resources, your organisation has to prioritise and focus on the products and customer segments that will drive the highest results. Second, while content marketing has been all the rage over the past few years, 70 % of marketers still complain that their content marketing is ineffective (Content Marketing Institute 2016). This is because of a variety of reasons—including lack of a content strategy and a lack of customer understanding, and what it really takes to influence their purchase decision. Third, internal marketing and sales alignment toward a common goal or initiative doesn't just happen. Significant coordination of resources must occur for companies to successfully implement a campaign or marketing initiative.

So let's take a look at how your organisation can implement a repeatable process in the ideation, creation and distribution of marketing campaigns.

The Elements of a Marketing Campaign

First, let's define what a marketing campaign is. Based on our research and experience, we've come up with the following definition: a *multi-faceted, end-to-end customer communications strategy, designed to execute against a key business objective.*

Marketing campaigns come in all shapes and sizes. Whether you're implementing a big initiative (such as a new product launch) or a small initiative (such as a local event), a successful marketing campaign has some shared characteristics:

* A designated campaign manager or project owner
* A clear goal and set of objectives that tie to broader corporate ambitions
* An identified target audience
* A clear campaign theme
* A compelling and creative message
* A measurable and flexible execution plan
* Internal collaboration and alignment

The ideal campaign also has a perfect blend of strategy and tactics. Strategy minus tactics is just big thoughts and no action. Tactics without strategy is plain chaos, a disaster waiting to happen. If you want your campaign to be a success, your strategy and tactics must work in absolute tandem.

So What's the Difference Between Strategy and Tactics?

A *strategy* is a plan for how a specific goal could be achieved, while a *tactic* is the action you take to achieve it. In other words, a strategy is the answer to what you're going to do to meet a goal; a tactic is how you're going to do it.

For example, if you want to increase your sales revenue, that's your goal. One of the ways you could achieve that goal is by driving more traffic to your website; that's your strategy. You could build landing pages, engage customers through social media, create email marketing campaigns and so on—and these would be deemed as tactics you could implement to execute the strategy you'd outlined.

Why Do You Need a Marketing Campaign Plan?

Marketing campaigns require a lot of discipline and work to pull off. With more pressure being put on the marketing team to prove their value, a marketing campaign plan helps put everyone on the same page and ensure that your marketing budgets are not being wasted.

Benefits of having a plan:

- *Aligns your marketing efforts to bigger corporate goals and priorities.* It's no secret that marketers continue to struggle with demonstrating their effectiveness. In fact, a survey by Fournaise Group in London (Fournaise Group 2012) found that 73 % of CEOs (chief executive officers) believe 'marketers lack business credibility and the ability to generate sufficient growth', and 80 % believe marketers are disconnected from short-, medium- and long-term financial objectives and realities. Ouch. And this is having an impact on customers as well: as we've covered in earlier chapters, 94 % of customers have tuned out from organisations who send them irrelevant content. Developing a plan forces you to think about how your marketing efforts will directly impact your organisation's goals, what your strategy is to achieve your goals and how you will measure and communicate your progress.
- *Keeps you focused.* There will always be something to distract you. Whether it's a new marketing technology or tool, a new sales opportunity or a new business partnership to evaluate, a plan ensures that you are staying focused on the big levers that will drive your business forward. And don't worry: you can add in some flexibility to take advantage of new opportunities, while insulating your organisation from all of the noise that is certain to come up.
- *Gets everyone on board.* How many times has your organisation tried and failed to execute a new initiative? A plan helps to ensure that you have the full support of your entire team (executives, marketing, sales, product, customer service, etc.) before moving into execution mode. This ensures that your resources are not wasted and that you don't run into internal roadblocks along the way.

Critical Roles to Success

Before we go into the step-by-step process of creating a campaign plan, it is necessary to discuss two pivotal roles in the planning process. The first is your campaign manager, who, like a conductor, leads the entire team toward achieving a common goal. As the lead project manager, s/he will oversee the entire process—gathering the right team members, assembling the campaign strategy, overseeing the planning, execution and reporting phases; responsible for regularly meeting the execution team to discuss progress, deliverables and any changes in direction.

The campaign manager typically resides within the marketing or product organisation. The campaign manager is usually very familiar with the business strategy, and what the organisation hopes to achieve with the campaign. S/he should also have a deep understanding of both customer needs and the buying/ selling process. This is important, as there will be times when a decision is needed during the planning process, and the campaign manager should be able to make a recommendation.

In working with several organisations, we have noticed that the campaign conductor is an often overlooked role, and yet the overall success of your campaign often resides on his/her shoulders. In a future book we will cover the skill sets and characteristics required for the modern marketing department. For now, here are some characteristics that a campaign manager should have:

- Strong communication and presentation skills
- Ability to be extremely organised and detail oriented
- Confidence and assertion
- Facility for listening and distilling the essence of what is being said
- Ability to collaborate and to get buy in from peers and superiors
- Risk management ability, foreseeing problems before they arise

The second role is proposition manager. Throughout the UK and Europe there has been a massive growth in this role. It was pioneered in the late 1990s by organisations such as BT and IBM. If you look on a job board, you can understand why we spent time in Chaps. 1 and 2 talking about clarifying definitions, as proposition manager roles vary a lot. The proposition manager is the person who helps pull together the complete company offer and messaging under the proposition themes. For example, there could be an 'agility' proposition manager. The proposition manager also helps to conduct and gather customer research and intelligence in order to fully understand customer needs and offer solutions to meet those needs.

In an ideal world, organisations should have both a campaign manager and a proposition manager.

The Planning Framework

We've broken the campaign planning process into two phases, as depicted in Fig. 7.1. During Phase 1, your job is to thoroughly research your market so that you understand your target audience, set realistic objectives and develop a plan that will break through the clutter and resonate with your target audience. During Phase 2, you will begin to execute the plan outlined in Phase 1, test and deploy marketing tactics and measure/analyse your overall impact.

Often, marketers want to jump to Phase 2 without spending sufficient time in Phase 1. Because, let's face it, it's a lot more fun to work on creating a new video, brochure, or email graphic than it is to research customer needs. But here's the catch. You *cannot* implement a campaign that drives customer engagement and increased sales activity if you do not properly plan it first. That would be like starting to build a house without waiting for the architectural drawings.

You'll also notice that we advocate setting up formal checkpoint meetings at the end of each step in order to keep all relevant parties informed of direction and progress. Depending on your organisation, these meetings may need to involve representatives from numerous departments. We believe internal communication cannot hurt!

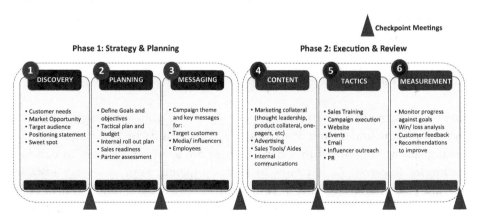

Fig. 7.1 Campaign planning framework

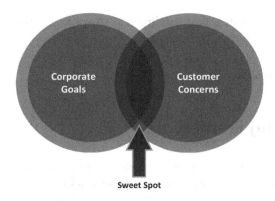

Fig. 7.2   Focus on the sweet spot

Phase 1

Discovery

Think of this as an information-gathering stage. The goal of the discovery phase is to form a view on how your campaign will tie together your organisation's internal objectives with what your target audience needs and expects from you. As Fig. 7.2 illustrates, the 'sweet spot' is where your offer overlaps with customer concerns.

Industry factors, your competitive advantage in the market, current events and profit margins can all affect which products receive a higher degree of focus. As we discovered in Chap. 5, you can promote a bunch of different products under one customer theme.

The discovery phase can be broken down into two parts—external and internal. Use the Discovery Questionnaire (Fig. 7.3) to help gather information.

External Discovery

It should come as no surprise that the success of your campaign hinges on how well you understand your target audience and the dynamics they are facing. As we've covered in Chap. 4, there are a variety of ways to conduct customer research. As it relates to your campaign, your discovery research should be even more specific to your campaign theme and objectives. In other words, your research here is trying to help answer and validate specific ques-

External Discovery	Internal Discovery	
Customer Needs and Pain Points	**Campaign Focus**	**Product Focus**
• Target audience description • Needs, pain points, motivations • Decision making unit • Decision making process	• What is the focus of this campaign? • How does this campaign support an immediate customer need/ pain point? • How does this campaign support our corporate objectives?	• Is our product uniquely positioned? • What is the overall product value proposition? • How is our product/ offer differentiated?
Market Opportunity	**Campaign Goals**	**Special offer**
• What is the current size of the market segment? • How are we positioned to compete? • Are there industry/ current events that make this a great opportunity?	• What are we trying to achieve? (KPI's) • What does "good" look like? • What is the budget for this campaign? • How will we measure success?	• Will we develop a special price, bundled package or promotional offer? • How does our offer compare to our competitors?
Competitive Landscape	**Recommended Reading**	**Sales Readiness**
• Who are our primary competitors? • What are our competitors saying in the market? • What is our ability to compete?	• Are there articles, reports or research that will help educate everyone on the customer/ situation?	• Is the Sales team prepared to take our story to the market? • What training is required to get the sales team ready?

Fig. 7.3 Discovery questionnaire

tions, rather than searching for patterns and broad insights. There are three key areas to look at:

1. *Customer needs and pain points.* Analyse current customer trends and internal data. For example, if you are planning to promote a specific set of products, look at where your sales team has been successful in selling these products. Talk to your customers directly to understand their current situation, pain points, motivations and needs related to your overarching theme and your firm's offer. Compare what your customers are saying to what your sales team is saying. Your goal is to walk away with a clear understanding of your customer's problem and how your company can help solve it.

2. *Market opportunity.* Recognising what is taking place in the industries you are targeting will help you intelligently position your firm's solution. Industry trends, drivers and headlines all play a factor into how much mindshare your message will ultimately receive. In the opening story featuring Jane, for example, the market situation highly impacted the relevance and timeliness of her campaign and message. If the stock market was soaring and performing well, her campaign message would have missed the mark.

3. *Competitive Landscape.* As we covered in Chap. 2, it is critical to understand what sets you apart from your competitors. During your campaign discovery phase, you should also become familiar with what your competi-

tion is doing from a marketing standpoint and which products they are trying to push. This will help inform your tactical marketing plans later.

Internal Discovery

The goal is to get your internal team focused and to ensure that they are aligned with the campaign objectives. Your campaign conductor should take the lead to interview key stakeholders across sales, product, executive leadership and marketing. The purpose of the interviews is to create a picture of what 'good' looks like. You need buy-in if you want to execute a successful campaign, and this is where it starts. This information, coupled with the broader market research you've been conducting (as outlined in Chap. 4), will give you a thorough understanding of which customers you are trying to reach, with what message and product set. You will also be able to assemble your campaign plan and objectives.

Going back to the story at the beginning of the chapter, Jane failed to gain alignment early in the campaign planning process. She was moving so fast that she didn't stop to include her sales and product teams in the planning process. She was clear about her marketing goals (increasing web traffic, email subscribers and webinar attendees), but she didn't go any further, to understand how these goals would *complement* or *compete with* other internal sales and product goals.

Your internal discovery should cover topics such as:

- Which overarching theme you are going to promote (for example, 'Efficiency')
- The primary target audience you are trying to reach
- Which product(s) you are going to focus on and whether or not your organisation is willing to create a special 'offer' (pricing discount, bundled package, extended trial, etc.)
- Your specific (versus aspirational) goals for this initiative

For example:
To create awareness and drive $x in new sales for our XYZ product.
To generate 500 new leads and 100 new sales opportunities within the next 90 days.
To be viewed as a thought leader in XYZ product category through analyst and press coverage.

- How you will measure success
- How this initiative will help achieve your corporate goals
- What stands in the way of success (i.e. lack of budget, resources, too many competing priorities, etc.)
- Is your sales team ready to sell this solution?

At the end of the discovery phase, we advise scheduling a checkpoint meeting to review the information you've collected with the broader team to gain agreement on moving forward to the next step.

Strategy and Planning

Once the high-level campaign direction is outlined, marketing should take the lead to determine *how* the campaign objectives are going to be met. This should of course be a collaborative process with the sales team, as they will ultimately have insight into what will work best and resonate the most with their customers. Conduct a subgroup conversation with the various constituents in marketing (branding, creative services, content writers, channel marketers, public relations, sales enablement, etc.) to discuss the best options and marketing tactics for the campaign. If you are working with a creative agency, this is a good time to start involving them.

Questions to ask during this stage:

- Which tactics are going to produce the best results?
- What is our media-worthy story? Who will be our face to the media?
- How will the sales team be the most energised and successful?
- How realistic is our goal? Should it be broken down into smaller objectives?
- How much budget do we have to support this initiative?
- Are there any other internal or external initiatives that we can leverage? Or that will compete with this initiative?
- How will we roll out the campaign internally?
- What are the key dates and timing for this campaign?

Use the template below (Fig. 7.4) to capture your campaign plan on one page.

At the end of this stage, host another checkpoint meeting to present the plan and seek input from your constituents.

Core Theme: (Choose from your top customer themes)			
Campaign goal: (Overarching campaign goal)			
Product Focus: (Which products/ services are you going to highlight during this campaign?)			
Target Audience description and decision maker profile: (Firmographics and Job titles/ departments)			
Objectives	**Approach**	**Measurement**	**Tactics**
Objective #1: Be specific and time-bound	Which marketing and sales levers will help drive this objective?	- How will you measure success against your goal?	- For example email campaign, webinars, events, sales training, etc.
Objective #2			
Objective #3			

Fig. 7.4 One-page campaign plan

Messaging

Most of the early chapters of this book have been dedicated to creating your perfect 'foundational' message, based on themes that will resonate with your customers. As it relates to your marketing campaign, you will build upon your foundational value proposition and refresh it, so it is timely and appropriate.

This is the opportunity to be more context-based (and relevant), by taking advantage of timely events or issues affecting your customer's world.

Questions to consider:

- Are there seasonal events or holidays that are relevant in your industry? Examples are tax day, big sporting events. We worked in organisations that were always rushing at the last minute to decide whether to do a campaign linked to the Super Bowl, even though it always took place the same time every year. In the same way we always seemed to be rushing to put something together for hurricane season. Although slightly less predictable, this always occurred at the same time of year.
- Are there industry or market events that you may want to reference? Examples are industry conferences, the ups and downs of the stock market.
- Has your industry made new strides or advances? This could also be new research that supports one position or another.
- Has the government implemented new regulations or legislature?

- Has there been turnover of top industry executives or influencers?
- What are our proof points?
  The answers to these questions will help you form a contextually based message for your campaign.

Let's build on the example that we raised in Chap. 5 about the neighbourhood restaurant. This is known for delivering 'a healthy dining experience by using only organic, locally sourced ingredients' (this is their foundational value proposition). At a time when the quality of our food is being questioned, this message really resonates with local residents. The restaurant has noticed a trend that more and more families with young kids are visiting. After some external research, they uncover that during the autumn, when kids head back to school, families are pressed for time in the evening and don't cook at home as much as they'd like. In order to take advantage of this opportunity, the restaurant runs a marketing campaign aimed at families during the busy back-to-school months. The goal is to be the first choice that comes to mind when parents think about taking their kids out for a healthy, quick meal.

Figure 7.5 illustrates how the campaign message supports the overall core theme and brand message, but is slightly tailored for this specific scenario and set of objectives.

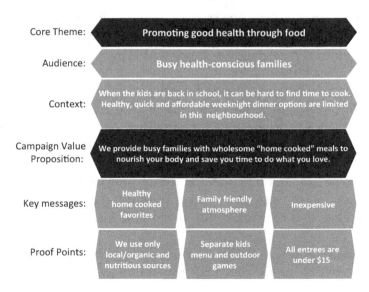

Fig. 7.5 Campaign messaging

Testing Your Message

At the end of the messaging phase, it is once again necessary to review your direction with the broader campaign planning team. Members of your sales team should be able to envision themselves delivering this message to their customers. We advise you to test your message with customers to ensure that it resonates and addresses their concern accurately. You can do this by enlisting the same customers you talked to during the discovery phase. You may also appoint a few sales representatives to deliver your message to customers in order to test their reaction and feedback.

Phase 2

Now that you have a solid strategy and plan in place, it's time to move on to execution. This is where all of your discovery and planning efforts pay off.

Content Creation

You've probably heard the advice to 'Give your customers content that is truly valuable'. But it can be hard to know exactly *what* to create that will help customers move along their journey with your company.

Unfortunately there's no magic bullet. But there *is* a model you can use to ensure that your content has a purpose.

First, your content should be created to address the various questions your prospect will have as s/he moves through the buying cycle. If your content is failing to address one of your customer's critical questions, then it risks being ineffective and a waste of time.

Next, focus on building trust and credibility with your content. What will entice your prospect to spend a few extra minutes learning about your company? The more you demonstrate your expertise and knowledge of your prospect's problem and situation, the more likely it is that s/he will agree to be courted by your company.

Last, remember the content preferences of your target audience. Do they like to consume videos or text-based articles? Are they analytical, preferring to see numbers and charts? Do they invest time in attending online or live events?

Refer back to Chap. 6 (Fig. 6.3) to determine the types of content you may want to produce to help your buyer during each stage of the journey.

Tactical Execution

Marketing tactics are constantly changing. You may have specialists in your organisation who are responsible for your website, social media, email, events, etc. Let them provide their advice and expertise when it comes to deploying these tactics, but stay focused on the overall plan. The important factors to keep in mind at this stage:

Keep Your Eye on the Ball Tactical execution requires a methodical approach and follow-through. It may take you several rounds of back and forth with the graphic designer or copywriter before you get everything 'just right'.

Gain Approval Along the Way The worst case scenario is going through weeks of development only to be shot down just before you cross the finish line. Set up internal checkpoint meetings and reviews so that your marketing leaders, sales representatives and product team can provide input along the way. In our experience, organisations tend to get caught up with the precise copywriting, so it's a good idea to start this process early.

It's also wise at this stage to remind everyone of the communications schedule and to review plans with your customer service and operations teams, to ensure that there aren't any routine maintenance plans scheduled that may compete with your plans.

Go with the Flow It's impossible to foresee every issue that may arise during the planning phase. As you start to move towards execution, you may realise that the plan you put in place can't be executed exactly as you'd envisioned. That's OK. Just remember to keep everyone informed and present new options to the planning team as these issues arise.

Measurement

Finally, it would be difficult to declare your campaign a success without properly measuring and monitoring results.

As internal priorities continue to shift, it's important not to lose sight of what you set out to accomplish with your campaign. The most effective way to monitor and communicate progress is to create a campaign dashboard that can be shared with the broader organisation.

As you'll likely be monitoring several different areas across the marketing-sales continuum, you may be quickly overwhelmed with data. Keep it simple, and highlight the overall progress and impact that your campaign is seeing. A campaign dashboard is an effective tool for communicating the progress of your campaign to the rest of the team. Be sure to include your original goals, so that you can track your progress along the way. You can organise your dashboard according to your primary objectives. For example:

- Generate awareness: PR coverage, ad impressions, website visitors, e-newsletter sign-ups
- Create engagement: social media engagement, email open rates/click-throughs, webinar attendance, event attendance
- Increase demand: new customer inquiries, qualified leads, sales meetings, new sales opportunities
- Contribute sales: new customers, average deal size, referrals, net promoter score, new revenue, profit margin, sales cycle time reduction

In addition to measuring your campaign quantitatively, it is also important to seek more qualitative feedback, such as:

- Conducting a win/loss analysis to determine why your firm is winning or losing deals. It is especially beneficial to talk to customers who have decided not to purchase from your firm.
- Seeking input from your sales team on how customer conversations are going and if your message/content is resonating with them.
- Interviewing new customers to better understand why they chose your firm over the competition.
- Reviewing reports and/or talk to third-party influencers, media and analysts to understand the reception in the marketplace to your message and offering.

Pitfalls to Avoid When Campaign Planning

Over the years, we've developed and taken to market A LOT of marketing campaigns. Here are some of the most common pitfalls we've seen:

- *Skipping the Discovery step.* The success of your marketing campaign lies in your ability to truly understand what your customers care about, and creating messages that will resonate with them. Without a thorough discovery investigation, you may miss critical information that can give your content depth and make it truly valuable. You may be tempted to shortcut the process by limiting your discovery to a couple of interviews with the sales team. But be very careful here, as you will certainly end up with an incomplete picture

- *Getting lazy and creating one single campaign message.* Not all buyers are alike. Don't make your marketing message so generic that it ends up reaching nobody. But don't overcomplicate things either. You can start by focusing on your top two buyer types, then add on from there once you're certain you can execute.
- *Rushing through the process.* Nobody appreciates how long it takes to put together a thoughtful marketing campaign. Executives are impatient. Everyone wants a quick win. This can cause your entire marketing and sales organisation to rush around, throw something together and haphazardly get something out the door. On average, based on our experience, you need about twelve weeks (or longer depending on the sophistication of your offer) to go through the end-to-end process.
- *Not having a clear campaign manager or conductor.* In consensus-driven, siloed organisations, it's hard to create buy in. Everyone seems to have their own ideas on what will move the needle. This misalignment often results in delays, to the point where you may never get anything published. Avoid this trap by first assigning a specific campaign owner who is skilled at driving projects forward. Second, make sure executive checkpoints are scheduled throughout each stage of the process. This provides a forum for each team leader to weigh in, share their input and make recommendations. Finally, remember that the campaign doesn't end once it's launched. Ongoing review of the campaign metrics is necessary to ensure that there aren't any holes/gaps in your plan and that your resources are being used wisely.
- *Setting unrealistic goals.* It's worth mentioning this again. Some campaigns try to do too much. It's important to recognise the difference between an aspirational 'brand-building' campaign and a more direct revenue-generating campaign. Your goals should be attainable and measurable.

In the next chapter, we will look at how this campaign planning approach can be applied to your account-based marketing efforts, or what we like to call 'campaigns for one'.

Further Reading

Parrish, M. (2014). Create marketing your customers can use. *Forrester Research*.

Content Marketing Institute. (2016). *B2B marketing: 2016 benchmarks, budgets, and trends—North America*.

Fournaise Group. (2012). *Annual survey: Global marketing effectiveness program*. London.

8

Driving Results Through Account-Based Marketing

In this chapter we will look at:

- Our definition of account-based marketing (ABM) related to the value stack
- The benefits of ABM
- How to choose the right accounts for an ABM programme
- A five-step framework to build your ABM plan
- Common pitfalls to avoid with ABM

This short chapter helps explain an account-based approach to marketing and why it may be beneficial for your organisation to adopt such an approach.

What Is Account-Based Marketing?

Account-based marketing (ABM), which has been growing in popularity over the past few decades, has become a bit of a buzz phrase lately. As technology continues to advance, the definition of ABM has taken on a much more narrow definition than the one we recognise and are advocating in this book. Marketers now have access to more real-time data about their customers than ever before (while they browse the product section of your website, for example). This makes it possible to target buyers on their terms with highly personalised messages and content. Many ABM technology compa-

© The Author(s) 2017
S. Kelly et al., *Value-ology*,
DOI 10.1007/978-3-319-45626-3_8

nies stop there, defining ABM as simply the ability to advertise to individual buyers across a variety of platforms (web, social, mobile, etc.). Let's call this view 'ABM.net'.

We argue that ABM is not just about the technology or the ability to personalise content and reach individual IP addresses—ABM demands that you understand and market to your customers in a way that is relevant and resonates with them. It's about truly understanding and delivering individual value to your customers—that is, the process we outline in this book!

Instead of trying to reach a lot of potential buyers with a broad and generic message, ABM attempts to connect with individual buyers as segments of one. You may be familiar with key account management (KAM), a recognised business-to-business (B2B) approach to managing strategic accounts, which was popularised by firms such as IBM and Xerox. KAM is a sophisticated and comprehensive approach that utilises data and analysis, and treats significant customer accounts as 'markets' of one in order to provide relevant and customised solutions and service to that customer. KAM is very much about face-to-face interaction.

Our view is that ABM is a complementary communications approach to KAM that harmonises marketing communications with account-level activity. ABM is about concentrating your marketing and sales efforts to reach a small number of important accounts in the top two layers of the value stack (introduced in Chap. 2). We believe ABM is a holistic, strategic approach that forces the sales and marketing teams to work together to better understand individual customer needs; and develop creative, personalised and highly relevant programmes to engage with them.

The Challenge

B2B purchases are become increasingly more complex and consensus-driven with an average of 5.4 decision makers and —four to six departments now involved in making the decision (CEB, LinkedIn). As a result, it is no longer feasible for sales to identify one 'champion' within a company who will shepherd the deal through completion. This new buying dynamic has left companies struggling to determine the best way to reach all buyers within an organisation and drive them toward a sale. Additionally, buyers are demanding personalisation and are no longer satisfied with a 'one size fits all' approach to marketing and sales.

As Professor Malcolm McDonald, author of several books on KAM and planning points out, customers are getting bigger and more sophisticated, and they want tailor-made solutions. Organisations that are looking to succeed in this new era of sophistication must seek and establish beneficial partnerships with their customers. Therefore, you can see how crucial it is to use care when selecting accounts for both KAM and ABM.

You may be wondering whether you should abandon all of your other marketing efforts to see if this new approach works. Our advice is to consider the following questions, as an integrated ABM approach requires commitment and integration of resources in order to pull it off.

Here are some questions to consider:

- Has your organisation identified who its ideal customer is? For example, which customers are most likely to need and purchase your solutions? Which customers are easy to do business with? Miller Heiman suggests looking at the demographics and psychographics of your customers, such as:
  - Size of target audience
  - Number of end users of your product
  - Age and condition of customers' present equipment
  - Distance between customer and you
  - Importance place on reputation in market
  - Ethical standards
  - Attitudes towards people
  - Openness to innovation
  - Relative importance quality v quantity
- Does your organisation have limited sales and marketing resources?
- Do you have customers who only buy a sliver of what your company sells?
- Are your sales cycles generally long and complex?
- Do you have to gain approval from multiple decision-makers before you make a sale?
- Do you wish you could better demonstrate the ROI of your marketing programmes?

It doesn't matter if your organisation is large or small. If you answered 'Yes' to the above questions, then your organisation could benefit from an ABM programme.

The Benefits of Implementing ABM

Account-based marketing is a fundamental shift from mass or broadcast marketing, whereby an organisation shouts a generic message to the market in hopes of creating *broad* awareness, to a narrower and more customised approach to create customer loyalty. ABM, by definition, is a highly targeted approach to reach your top accounts.

According to ITSMA, a B2B marketing research firm, a recent study found some of the following benefits associated with implementing an ABM programme:[1]

- 84 % of companies said ABM delivers higher return on investment (ROI) than other marketing initiatives
- 76 % said ABM helped customers view their organisation as more credible and trustworthy
- 57 % said sales was able to uncover more opportunities within accounts
- 57 % increased account penetration (wallet share, revenue and margin)
- 48 % said sales was able to have more meaningful conversations with customers

In our own experience, one technology organisation we worked with implemented a tightly knit and strategic ABM programme. The marketing and sales leaders worked closely together to first identify a list of ideal targets based on possible opportunity size, current spend, location and propensity to purchase. Then they established key objectives, such as expanding the number of contacts within the account, developing stronger relationships with executives and selling more broadly across the portfolio.

The result? Record year-on-year growth and deeper sales and marketing alignment (because each team was working toward a common set of account objectives).

How Do I Get Started?

Here we provide the fundamentals—a five-step framework (Fig. 8.1) that you can use to implement a successful ABM programme. As marketing technology is constantly changing, we will let you do the research to determine

---

[1] ITSMA (5 October 2015) *ABM Metrics: What's behind the numbers?* Lexington, MA. [online] Available at: http://www.itsma.com/event/abm-metrics-whats-behind-numbers/

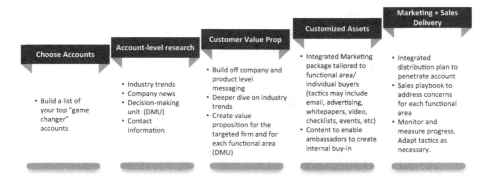

Fig. 8.1 Moving the sale forward: A 5 step framework

the best technology partner. But beware, there is a danger in using this new technology if you haven't first done the work to create relevant and resonate value propositions for your target audience, and if your marketing team is still pushing out unhelpful and product feature-led content.

Choosing the Right Accounts

Start by identifying your ideal customer list. When you get to the top of the value stack you need to make a clear decision about who your most important customers are. We advise that you select strategic accounts where 'mutual value' is achieved, which is to say that both your organisation and the customer benefit from the greater use of your products and services, resulting in a valuable partnership.

This should also be a relatively small list—for example, your top 100 'game changers'. Many firms will have a pareto effect, whereby 80 % of their revenue is generated by 20 % of their customers. For example, one of our clients, a large telecommunications firm, generates £2bn of revenue from ten customers, while the remaining 2500 customers make up £6bn revenue.

Think of it this way. If these accounts were to continue to do business with your firm, or become new customers, your organisation would see significantly more revenue, more industry credibility and easier access to other desirable prospects.

Each company will define their ideal customer differently, but here are some criteria to think about:

- Which companies are naturally aligned to what you have to offer?
- Which companies would benefit the most from your products/services?

- Which companies will value your services and expertise the most?
- Do you have a special niche that you are trying to grow?
- Which customers are the most profitable for your company? Is this based on location, size, who they serve, etc.?
- Are there existing accounts where you have very little share of wallet, but where you believe your customers could greatly benefit from your offer?

Account-Level Research

In Chap. 4 we discussed techniques to identify customer themes and triggers. As it relates to ABM, you will apply these same techniques to get at the heart of what is affecting your *specific* customer. This is a much deeper dive at the account level, and individual buyers and departments that will be involved in the decision.

This research is complementary to your KAM plan or traditional sales account planning.

During the research stage, you will want to understand and document what is happening in the world of your accounts, so that you can develop a tailored message and method to reach and engage with them.

Some areas to review:

- Company news—press releases, annual reports, social media posts
- Competitor review—website, press releases
- Industry reports—media, trade and analyst publications
- Contact databases—LinkedIn, Data.com, NetProspex, etc.
- Social media profiles—who are the likely decision-makers? What can you learn about them: favourite sports teams, etc.

You will also want to begin to piece together the decision-making unit (DMU), which is a specific list of every person in the organisation who will be involved in the purchasing decision. Be sure to include their name, title, contact details and especially the role they play in the decision-making process. The more personalised information you can find, the better. For example, one sales leader we work with makes it a habit to ask questions about his customers' favourite sports teams, as this provides great insight when you want to determine how to connect with a customer on a deeper level.

Customer Value Proposition

Most of this book has been dedicated to helping you create tailored value propositions. For ABM to be successful, you will need to create a value proposition that is specific to the company you are trying to reach. You will also need to craft tailored messages for each member of the DMU. Your objective is to demonstrate that you understand what your customer is trying to achieve and to articulate how your solution will help them. Use the frameworks introduced in Chap. 2 to build out your specific customer value proposition.

We drew this out at an opportunity level in Chap. 2, when we looked at different value propositions by a chief executive officer (CEO) for a call centre purchase (Fig. 2.3). Another example is a major blue-chip organisation, whose overarching value proposition is to help their customers 'create up to 30 % more efficiency in their day-to-day business operation'. Think about how this message shifts slightly to appeal to the different departments involved in the decision, such as the head of Customer Service ('Now you can improve customer response time by 15 %') and the VP of Finance ('Our solution enables you to cut business expenses by almost 15 %').

We have mentioned sessions where account teams were encouraged to bring in press clippings of company news to explore how new value propositions could be developed. We saw in an earlier chapter how this led to the sale of a web security system after a cyber attack.

Customised Assets and Offers

The more personalised your marketing message, materials and offers, the more likely you are to break through the clutter and reach your prospective buyer. This is where your creativity comes in. How will you stay in front of your prospect with a consistent, compelling and relevant message? For example, one company that we worked with created tailored direct mail packages using publicly available information that showed where their prospect's employees were around the USA and how their telecommunication services could be connected to each location to enable a more efficient work stream. They sent these packages to executive decision-makers, which led to an increase in sales activity and meetings.

As we outlined in Chap. 3, the unique voice of the sales person should be captured here too, in order to deliver a highly customised proposition in the right tone and on the right theme.

Our view is that your ABM programme needs to be built for the long haul, at least six to twelve months, and should incorporate a variety of marketing and sales tactics (online and offline) designed to connect with buyers, introduce how you can help and advance the sales process.

Remember that your buyer interacts with your firm in a variety of ways—online, mobile, events, in person meetings and so on. So think about your strategy from all angles.

For complex sales, one of the most powerful assets that you can create is something your customer can share between departments, and answers the most common questions related to their problem (and how you can help them solve it). E-books, white papers and videos are popular because they are easily shareable. In fact, 91 % of executives said they would happily forward marketing content if they found it insightful and relevant (Corporate Executive Board).

Marketing and Sales Delivery

Perhaps more so than other marketing methods, ABM helps to ensure that there is an integrated plan of attack between sales and marketing to reach your targeted accounts. More specifically, you will need to define exactly what success looks like so that both teams are clear on the direction of the programme. For example, are you trying to increase the number of contacts within an account? Build stronger relationships with the C-suite? Improve your win rate? Impact revenue growth? And so on.

Because the marketing plan is being developed at the account level, the sales department directly benefits from customer outreach at the top layers of the value stack, and is eager to play an active role in providing feedback and follow-up.

There are several marketing technology companies that allow you to do account-based advertising—targeting your individual buyer online and in real time using their IP address. This is a critical new component that allows you to reach and remind your buyers about your firm as they are conducting their own online research. In addition, direct mail, email and telemarketing are a great way to reach individual customers and aim to learn more about their business and secure a meeting for sales. As you are starting to build a relationship with your top ideal prospects, you may want to consider focusing additional company resources, such as members of your executive leadership team, to help reach these individuals and demonstrate your commitment. For example, CEO to CEO outreach can be very effective and powerful as a genuine way to connect with new prospects and demonstrate trust and credibility.

As it relates to reaching and strengthening existing customer relationships, in addition to collecting data from website visits, offline tactics can also be extremely powerful. For example, we've worked with several organisations that have had success hosting executive round table discussions, which are designed to facilitate neutral conversations at a more strategic level (without necessarily having all the answers), and can lead to beneficial insights.

As the goal of ABM is to build solid relationships with your top customers and prospects, it is also important to ensure that your sales team is ready to discuss your value proposition and tailor the conversation for each member of the decision-making unit when the time comes. Several of our clients choose to equip their sales teams with a messaging 'playbook' to help them navigate these conversations. The playbook generally includes a description of the customer, their business problems, business-related questions to ask, customer examples and case studies, and a clearly articulated value proposition by functional area.

Lastly, we recommend setting up a formal review process to discuss progress on each account and what's working/not working. As you learn more about each of the accounts that you are trying to reach, it is critical to continue to evolve your programme, messaging and tactics to ensure relevance and resonance at the customer level.

Common Pitfalls with Account-Based Marketing

As you start to build out your ABM programme, here are some common pitfalls to avoid.

Sales and Marketing Are Not Aligned

In order for your ABM programme to be successful, sales and marketing have to be on the same page. This is often a problematic area for organisations, who continue to operate business as usual and expect different results. Outline your goals and objectives for the programme and ensure that both departments are in agreement on the target customer list, messaging and outreach plans. And crucially, make sure that both parties are involved in the entire five-step framework that we've outlined above. Otherwise, you could end up like one company we know, whose sales team selected accounts for the ABM programme without marketing's involvement—ignoring key data, inputs and analysis that ultimately required them to go back to account selection well after the programme was supposed to be under way. We will go into more detail on sales and marketing alignment in Chap. 9.

Trying to Go After Too Many Accounts

Given the labour-intensive nature of ABM, we advise starting with a small number of accounts. You may be tempted to breeze through the customer research phase and start sending generic marketing content and messages to all prospects within a particular industry. Don't do it. This will just water down your message and get your marketing materials sent straight to the rubbish bin.

Creating a 'One Size Fits All' Package

We know that it can be time consuming to create customised marketing materials. If you've followed our methodology so far you should be in good shape. Before you've got to this point, you'll have developed themes and an industry-level view on major issues and opportunities. Our version of ABM at the top end of the value stack demands that you take a deeper dive at customer and individual level to create value propositions that are highly relevant and tailored.

Giving Up Too Early

Your organisation will get tired of the programme long before your prospects do. We have seen many organisations give up and move on as other internal priorities and pressures arise. Instead of throwing in the towel, implement a methodical process to evaluate the programme's success and discuss how to evolve your messaging and tactics to stay relevant and impactful.

Starting in Isolation

Starting at the account level is a legitimate tactic, and is certainly an approach we have witnessed. If you do this in isolation, however, then you risk letting your broader organisation pull the value rug from under your feet with irrelevant product push messages.

Again we would cite the senior information technology marketer we originally met in Chap. 2, who waxed lyrical about her ABM programme. When asked what set her organisation apart from competitors she said, 'Nothing, it's a commoditised industry.'

So, make sure all the key players in your marketing and sales departments are brought into the programme, starting at value theme level.

Successful ABM relies entirely on clear, aligned value proposition articulation and close co-cooperation with sales and key account managers who service accounts on a daily basis.

We all know how difficult it can be getting marketing and sales to work in harmony, a topic we now turn to.

Further Reading

McDonald, M., & Woodburn, D. (2011). *Key account management: The definitive guide* (3rd ed.). Chichester: Wiley.

9

Align or Die? Ensuring Marketing and Sales Are Aligned with the Customer

In this chapter we will look at:

- Why it is increasingly important for marketing and sales to align with the customer
- What the latest research says about the state of alignment today
- A methodology for testing how well aligned your organisation is
- Providing a path forward for developing greater alignment to drive improved performance in the marketplace

Crucially you will have a clear diagnosis of alignment in your own company and a clear plan to develop greater alignment.

All of what we have covered so far can live or die on perhaps the most controversial issue we have tackled—marketing and sales alignment. From our perspective it's not just a question of whether marketing and sales are aligned; it's ultimately about customer alignment. This chapter helps you work out how well aligned your marketing and sales are to the customer. By the end of it you should have a clear plan for getting aligned, so as to execute the approach prescribed in this book.

© The Author(s) 2017
S. Kelly et al., *Value-ology*,
DOI 10.1007/978-3-319-45626-3_9

Definition of Alignment

The definition of alignment we will run with in this chapter is:

Noun alignment
  1: the act of aligning or state of being aligned; *especially*: the proper position-ing or state of adjustment of parts (as of a mechanical or electronic device) in relation to one another
  2: an arrangement of groups or forces in relation to one another
  Source: 'alignment'. Merriam-Webster.com 2016

The Approach

In this chapter we will be 'eating our own dog food' by modelling the approach we put forward for understanding customers and markets in Chap. 4. We will begin by examining a combination of secondary commercial research and academic research into marketing and sales alignment. After this we will cover the results of our own original research: an alignment survey we sent to over 120 marketing and sales practitioners and in-depth interviews with fifty marketing and sales leaders.

We will then provide you with a tool to help you assess how well your organisation is aligned right now. Finally we will put forward a prescription to achieve customer alignment that drives revenue and sales growth.

Why Is Alignment Important?

Quite simply, highly aligned organisations achieve better results. According to a 2011 Aberdeen Group study, highly aligned organizations achieved an aver-age of 32 % year-on-year revenue growth, while their less aligned competitors saw a 7 % decrease in revenue. Yet according to a Forrester study, just 8 % of companies say they have tight alignment between sales and marketing.

Indeed, a number of recent pieces of business research seem to indicate that this lack of alignment is prevalent. A survey by recruitment specialist Randstad entitled 'The divide between sales and marketing' (2015) found that, despite 80 % of UK businesses recognising the benefits of greater align-ment between sales and marketing, 40 % still have no systems in place to unify the functions. The biggest barriers to integrating a strategy to bring marketing and salespeople closer together included perceived rigid organisa-tion structures (cited by 34 %) and corporate culture bias towards sales and marketing roles (26 %).

In *Frugalnomics* Tom Pisello (2015) points to Sirius Decisions' research (2014), which found that 32 % of salespeople lacked useful or relevant content from marketing. In *Aligning Strategy and Sales* Frank Cespedes (2014) reminds us that 'Studies indicate that less than 40 % of firms believe sales and marketing are aligned with what their customers want', the very reason for alignment.

So, sales and marketing alignment still appears to be a problem at a time when it matters more than ever. In this omni-channel era when potential buyers get lots of product and company information online, Pisello (2015) points out that 67 % of buyers have a clear picture of the solution they want before they engage a sales rep (Sirius Decisions 2014). At the same time, 94 % of potential customers have disengaged with vendors because they received irrelevant content (Corporate Executive Board research).

Nothing much seems to have changed at the sales and marketing interface (SMI) since the seminal *Harvard Business Review article* 'Ending the war between sales and marketing' (Kotler et al. 2007), despite the heightened significance of the consequences of misalignment.

Alignment Issues: What Does the Academic Research Say?

There are a number of themes that come out of the SMI literature. Here we will focus on three, economic and goal differences, cultural differences, cognitive or 'thought world' differences, together with sales 'buy-in' to marketing strategy.

Economic Differences

These really begin with budget allocation. With resources scarce not all marketing and sales activity asks will be fully funded. Kotler et al. (2007) also point to tensions inherent in the marketing mix, or 7Ps of marketing, which are Product, Price, Promotion, Place, Physical Evidence, Process and People (7Ps). From a price standpoint marketing sets the list price while sales can go straight to the chief financial officer for sign-off on individual bids. With regard to promotion, sales can be critical of where money is spent, and can contrast this with the relevance of marketing material provided to them, as we saw earlier in the research. The vice-president of sales might prefer extra salespeople to money being spent on advertising or brand building activity. Goals and incentives can also be at odds. While sales are rewarded for hitting sales and revenue targets for a set of customers, marketers could be incentivised for achieving programme goals that don't tie directly to sales goals. Product marketers tend to have profit and loss as a key metric while sales are focused on volume.

Cultural Differences

Studies by Beverland et al. (2006) sought to understand cultural differences between marketing and sales. They examined the question of 'cultural frames' to test if these resulted in tension. The definition of culture was one that consisted of mental frames by which we approach behaviour, and they examined differences in key cultural assumptions.

In their work *Cultural Frames that drive Sales and Marketing apart (2006: 386–394)* they identified four cultural frames:

- *Valid scope of focus and activity*—sales are focused on a single, or small group of customers, while marketers look after a market
- *Time horizons*—sales are focused on short-term immediate customer needs. Marketing are more long-term focused and pay little regard to day-to-day customer problems.
- *Valid sources of knowledge*—marketing only see sales as a valid source of short-term, individual customer information, not for anything more strategic.
- *Relationship to environment*—sales perceptions and practice identify the importance of reacting to customer requirements. Marketing is concerned with driving the marketplace to increase margin and sources of growth.

Bringing this discussion up to date, Cespedes (2014) cleverly describes marketing and sales as 'alone together'. In addition, he points out that because of scope differences, sales will want to customise for an individual customer, which may not suit marketing. Interestingly, though, Rouzies and Hulland (2014) found that where customer concentration is low, sales and marketing can align to support a big spending customer in a way that may not be beneficial to their organisation. They put this down to a power imbalance that many business-to-business (B2B) people will have experienced.

Problems arise owing to conflicting priorities or 'dialects', or what is considered to be core activity in daily routines. Over time these determine 'how things are done around here', leading to 'Esperanto silos' where sales and marketing operate as separate entities (Cespedes 2014).

Cognitive 'Thought World' Differences: On the Same Wave-Length?

Homburg and Jensen (2007) sought to understand whether differences between 'thought worlds' of marketing and sales are beneficial or not. They considered how differences in world view would help or hinder the enactment of marketing decisions, with relation to marketing and sales. Their investigation revealed that, in general, differences hamper cooperation between marketing and sales that leads to lower performance. Some facets of thought world differences enhance performance through a direct effect that outweighs the negative effect of quality of cooperation.

There are contradictory views on the nature of thought world differences. Some have called for similar thought worlds (Donath 1999). Others have supported differences, for example, Cespedes (1996) "The solution is not to eliminate differences among these groups".

Homburg and Jensen (2007) found that different thought worlds can have a positive effect. Competency differences are bad as they adversely affect performance. Differences among interpersonal skills and the knowledge funds of marketing and sales pose an interpretive barrier that gets in the way of optimal decision-making.

Sales 'Buy-in' of Marketing Strategies

Another topic that the academic literature explores is the need for the sales team to be brought into marketing strategies. We already saw what happened to Jane, the Financial Services Marketing Leader, who failed to get sales buy-in to her campaigns, so why is this buy-in important?

Salespeople are boundary spanners, and play a crucial role in ensuring that firms implement their strategies appropriately (Malshe and Sohi 2009).

At times distrust and prejudices at the interface make it difficult for each function to appreciate the other's role in the strategic process (Homburg et al. 2008). Where marketing does not involve sales in strategy development they may view the initiatives as ineffective or irrelevant (Kotler et al. 2006). This will mean the sales function does not buy into or support the initiatives proposed (Yandle and Blythe 2000).

Malshe and Sohi (2009) found that getting sales buy-in consisted of four key components; these are summarised in Fig. 9.1.

Components of buy-in	Key facets
1. Objectivity and Rational Persuasion	Help Sales the see the rationale behind a strategy was seen to be important so they can see the "why" - not treating them as pure executors
2. Sensitivity and responsiveness to reality	When marketers appreciate their different world-view from salespeople (Homburg and Jensen 2007; Panigyrakis and Veloutsu 1999; Workman et al. 1998) appreciate sales people's field experience, and responded appropriately, they were more open to what the marketers were telling them
3. Involvement in strategy creation	Marketing should involve Sales in the Strategy process and be prepared to negotiate from different points of orientation (Cespedes1996; Strahle et al.1996)
4. Positioning for success	Sales is looking for Marketing to position them for success that gives them a competitive advantage in the field. Even though sales want marketers to take on board their feedback and give input to the strategy, achieving sales objectives is an important focus (Carpenter 1992; Lorge 1999)

Fig. 9.1   Components of sales buy-in (Adapted from Malshe and Sohi (2009))

The notion of 'buy-in' integrates some of the earlier themes into the four stages proposed by Malshe and Sohi. Cespedes (2014) makes a compelling case for the need to align strategy and sales. The challenge is engaging sales-people, 'where the rubber hits the road', with strategists, 'where the rubber meets the sky'.

From what we can see from research results, it appears that 'buy-in' is much more difficult to achieve in practice. As an ex-Managing Director at BT used to say, 'It sounds simple, but it ain't easy.' How do you get alignment? Which shared processes need to be developed? How do you effectively share information? These are all questions that practitioners seem to be wrestling with. Crucially, the customer does not seem to be getting a coherent story from marketing and sales.

The good news is that this chapter is about giving you some answers to these alignment questions. After we have looked at our own research we will present a framework, with some helpful templates, to help you create a path towards top-quality alignment.

Survey Results

From our perspective we felt there did not seem to be much research into how well aligned marketing and sales were to the customer in relation to creating and developing value propositions. With this in mind, we performed our own primary research.

In the first piece of research we surveyed over 120 sales and marketing practitioners who were mainly based in the USA and UK, many of whom serve a global customer base. We asked a bunch of questions that were designed to test for alignment, with some interesting results that we have summarised in Fig. 9.2.

Why Do Customers Buy from You?

It seemed to us to be Alignment 101 that organisations should be clear why customers buy from them. We found that while 67 % of salespeople felt they were completely clear, 64 % of marketers said they were only somewhat clear. So what is happening with this 'why buy' gap?

This, in part, could be explained by the cultural differences outlined earlier around 'valid scope of focus'. Sales are focused on a single customer or a small group of customers, and they feel that it is clear why customers buy from them in their narrow context. Something seems to be happening that is preventing marketers from gaining this clarity across the broader market scope they have to deal with.

It seems that marketers are not helping themselves, as 21 % of salespeople said they were never asked to provide input to marketing about what's important to customers. Is this because marketers do not regard sales as a 'valid source of knowledge' for 'strategic' information on what customers regard as important, or why they buy from you or somebody else? Whatever the reason, there does seem to be a clear link between the 'why buy' gap and gaining sales input.

What Sets You Apart from Competitors?

There was a similar gap in relation to competitor understanding. While 45 % of marketers said they were only somewhat clear or not clear at all about what sets their organisation apart from competitors, 66 % of salespeople do feel clear about this.

QUESTION	MARKETING	SALES	TAKE-OUT
Is your organisation clear about why your customer choose to buy from you?	64% said they were only somewhat clear	67% said they were very or completely clear	Why is there such a big disconnect in clarity between sales and marketing?
How often do you marketing team ask you for input about what's important to customers?		21% said they never get ask for input	Maybe this goes some way to explaining the disconnect above
Is it clear what sets your organisation apart from competitors?	45% said they were somewhat clear or not clear at all	66% said they were clear about what sets them apart	Why is there such a big disconnect in clarity between sales and marketing?
Does your frim have a clear value proposition?	40% said they were only somewhat clear	58% said they were either somewhat or not clear	Is this because it gets harder as you get closer to the customer?
How effective is your content marketing?	75% said only somewhat effective		Look below for your answer!
What % of collateral produced by marketing do you actually use?		81% said they use 25% or less	
How effective is the collateral produced by marketing?		64% said somewhat or not effective	
Is it clear which marketing assets your sales team values and uses most?	75% said somewhat clear or not clear at all		
How well aligned is your marketing and sales to what the customer wants?	48% said only somewhat aligned	41% said only somewhat or not aligned	
How involved is sales when creating new content?	50% said only somewhat involved or not at all 20% not involved at all	73% said only somewhat or not involved 27% said not involved at all	Not much involvement but sales feel less involved than they even marketing feels they are

Fig. 9.2 Alignment survey results

Again, these could be seen as cultural differences, which are explained by sales having a narrow scope of focus and marketing not using sales as a 'valid source of knowledge' in relation to competitor activity.

In both these examples there does not appear to be any sort of closed loop. From a competitor standpoint we believe that through research, including input from sales, marketing should be declaring what they feel sets their organisation apart from competitors. This should be driven by factors that are important to customers. What then becomes important is that there is a constant flow of feedback from the marketplace via sales and other channels that allows competitive positioning to be reviewed. This does not seem to be happening.

Does Your Firm Have a Clear Value Proposition?

There does not appear to be much confidence around this question, as 40% of marketers and 58 % of salespeople said they were only somewhat clear.

The marketers' lack of confidence relates to how resonant the value proposition is with customers and how easily and widely they think the value proposition can be recited. The fact that sales are less clear shows that the nearer you get to the customer the harder it is to craft a value proposition, as it has to completely resonate with the issues the unique customer faces.

How Useful Is Content?

We asked 'mirror' questions here to understand how marketers felt about their content marketing, and to understand how sales felt about collateral provided to them by marketing. The results were interesting to say the least, amplifying the results found in the commercial surveys mentioned earlier.

From a marketing standpoint, 75 % felt that their content marketing was only 'somewhat effective'. The same percentage of marketers was either somewhat clear or not clear about which marketing assets the sales team valued and used most.

Mirroring this view, when we asked what percentage of collateral produced by marketing was actually used by sales we found that 81 % of salespeople used only 25 % or less, while 64% of salespeople felt that the collateral produced by marketing was either somewhat or not effective.

What may be perpetuating this is that 50 % or marketers said that sales were only 'somewhat involved' or 'not involved' when creating new content.

One in five marketers said that did not involve sales at all; while 73% of sales-people felt they were at best 'somewhat involved' and 27 % said they had no involvement in content creation whatsoever.

This is clearly a problematic area, which we have covered in Chap. 6 in some depth. Later on we will provide some tips for 'content' alignment.

What Do Current Practitioners Say?

We spend a lot of time talking with sales and marketing practitioners like you about alignment with the customer, as we are interested in helping you solve this problem. It seems that practitioners perceive this to be a big issue. In order to improve our understanding we hold in-depth interviews lasting up to an hour to try and understand 'what's happening out there'. What we hear could fill a book like this in its own right. We wanted to pick out some direct quotes from senior sales and marketing people that represent the themes emerging from our discussions. We're sure that these quotes will trigger thoughts about how things work in your organisation.

We will use these to help inform our approach for improving alignment in your organisation.

Goal Alignment: Enabler or Tension Point

"At the highest level I think it's about goal alignment. So typically the sales team has got sales goals and revenue sales goals that the marketing team doesn't necessarily always have. So the further you can push those same revenue goals down into the marketing organisation, the better you are from an alignment perspective."

Senior Vice-President of Marketing, global organisation

"You have marketers saying we generated 4000 MQLs, which translated into 500 SQLs and you guys dropped the ball on lots of them. And so you've got the *tension point* of the ability to translate the marketing work into tangible sales."

President, global high-tech company

"I think shared objectives are a big enabler. You know, shared objectives that are tied to compensation. If a sales and a marketing person has the same objective that leads to similar compensation reward that is a big enabler in our business."

Sales Vice-President, global technology company

It would seem to be a good starting point, pre-requisite or enabler to overall alignment that marketing and sales goals should be in sync. These can become true enablers if there's some synergy between marketing and sales compensation. In other words, if we meet these shared goals we'll all succeed. The issue here is that marketers do not always have shared goals with sales. This can become what the President of the global high-tech company articulately calls a 'tension point'. Sometimes marketers are overtly focused on goals around 'awareness' and 'interest' that relate to the broad end of the sales funnel. At a campaign level this can bring about too much emphasis being placed on leads that were generated and passed to sales, often referred to as MQLs (marketing qualified leads) or SQLs (sales qualified leads). This can lead to finger-pointing, as sales throws doubt on lead quality while marketing accuses sales of 'dropping the ball' or not having the ability to close their awesome leads.

Surely the point is that nothing has really happened until a sale has been made; the ultimate measure of success? Or is it? On the other hand how can you expect to make an instant sale to a potential customer who has never really heard of you? We worked with an organisation which was challenging much more well-known players in its field and only had around 20 % unprompted recall of who they were, let alone what they did. We would certainly advocate that at least at vice-presidential level there should be shared revenue and sales goals with shared rewards. Further down the organisation, marketers who are responsible for certain customer markets and segments should also share these goals. This has be underpinned with some role clarity, as there will be some parts of marketing that are responsible for improving that 20 % awareness score as a facilitator towards ultimate sales success. So how do practitioners feel about role clarity?

Role Alignment: Are We All in Sync?

'Tactical' Campaign and Lead Management Roles

> "If we're going to invest dollars in creating demand and generating leads, we need a formal commitment from sales that that they are going to work with us to create a formal lead definition that they're going to agree to pick up these leads within a certain timeframe; a little bit more tactical than the value proposition stuff but nonetheless, an important part of continuing to create that sales and marketing alignment."
>
> Director, Campaign Management, global company

Sticking with the more 'tactical' issue of leads, here we have a case in point where the primary role of this Marketing Director is to generate leads. People in these roles may be too overtly rewarded for the lead generation aspect of their job. For the core part of the role there has to be a clearly agreed process on what constitutes a good lead, with some commitment to follow up and provide feedback.

> "I have inherited a situation where all my sales scorecards are red and my marketing scorecards are green. That cannot be right'"
>
> Divisional President, global organisation

What this cannot lead to is a situation where marketing scorecards are green, because they've hit the goals for leads while sales is having difficulty converting them. For sure, we would recommend that marketing campaign management and sales have to sit down and agree the lead process and roles within that process. Beyond this there has to be a joint commitment to review the whole 'funnel' end to end, with an eye on the main overall goal, which is closing business.

Information and Conversation Flow

"In terms of the alignment between marketing and sales, if you think about drawing a line of sight from the people in the product marketing teams who build the services and then market them and take them to market through the sales organisation into the end customer, there's quite often a strong disconnect there. And if they do talk, they'll talk about new product launches and I guess at that point they may have some salespeople involved in that team, but predominantly they don't."

Sales Vice-President, global blue chip

There's a lot in this quote! Our major take-out is one that has been a constant theme of our conversations with sales and marketing practitioners. Almost everyone we talk to acknowledges that the main source of conversations between the two organisations is tactical. In this case it's about product marketing talking to sales only when they have a new product launch because they need them to sell the new product. Equally it could be sales saying to marketing "When is the next customer event? "or "When are more leads coming through?". This quote seems to emphasise that there's no real conversation about customer value here. In order to move from a product push to a customer centric organisation there needs to be more dialogue about what's important to customers.

Sales teams are stretched and they never really wanted to volunteer or to create value propositions and sit on internal committees when they could be out meeting with their customers. So there was definitely a balance of feedback for that.

Director of Marketing, US financial services

So there has to be some effort put towards gaining role clarity with regard to information flow, especially around customer value. To be effective this has to involve sales, who we know from our survey don't feel as if they're being consulted. It also has to recognise that taking salespeople 'off the road' should not be done lightly; all the more reason to be clear about roles around information and conversation flows. Crucially these need to lead to tangible improvements in value propositions.

Overall, what we recommend for the whole value proposition development process is that both 'sides' should sit down and agree 'duties' and 'rights'. A duty is something that relates to the core elements of what you do in your job. For example, a marketing communications manager has a duty to provide collateral to help support sales conversations with customers. The sales team may feel they have a 'right' to provide input to collateral development. Below is a sample selection of 'duties' and 'rights' for a B2B account manager which we have adapted from a client assignment:

Account Manager Duties

- To sell our products and services to customer base
- Update customer relationship management system with customer information
- Respond to marketing leads in agreed timescale
- Develop growth plans for customer accounts
- Complete paperwork for customer orders

Account Manager Rights

- Up-to-date information on products and services
- To expect updates on customer trends and issues
- High-quality, well-qualified leads
- Marketing programmes supporting growth plans
- Easy-to-use systems for order input

Role Clarity and the 'Sophistication' Gap

Yeah, I mean I think generally speaking there is a sophistication gap and certainly you'll hear from sales that I need use cases, I need references, I need a translation of your insights into actionable discussions. And I think the argument is whose responsibility is this to create those actionable discussions. And I think it's a joint responsibility.

President – global high-tech company

We like this gap most of all, not because it exists but rather because one of our insightful clients came up with a great name for it: 'sophistication gap'. What he meant by this, in the broader context, goes way back to our 'soap-bar' diagram in Chap. 2. We present a new version below, Fig. 9.3, that includes the 'sophistication gap'.

In Chap. 2 we outlined that at the bottom of the 'value stack' marketing has to undertake research, appropriately involving sales input, to understand the key business issues faced by customers. From this they develop proposition themes which become the platform to facilitate a customer centric communications approach. These become more resonant with customers as you move towards the top of the stack. The issue is that you have to traverse the 'sophistication gap'. The value propositions become more real when you start to discuss them with customers. Hopefully you'll be using sales dexterity during customer meetings to develop value 'in the moment' with the customer, as we discussed in Chap. 3. Here the value propositions have to be more 'sophisticated' as they have to resonate and be relevant to your customer, or the 5.4 customers that are involved in the decision making process. At this point the salesperson needs to have 'actionable insights'. Said differently, "This is what we can do for you (value proposition) and here is an example of where we've done this before (case study)."

Our client is absolutely right; it's a joint responsibility. During our interviews we've heard numerous sales leaders say that much of the material they

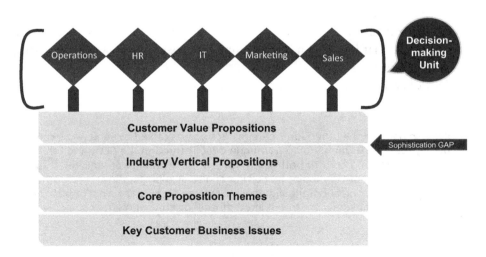

Fig. 9.3 Sophistication gap

got from marketing was 'too generic' to use with customers. From our standpoint, as you traverse the 'sophistication gap' towards the customer it's mainly a sales responsibility to make the value propositions come to life and resonate with customers. Marketers need to embrace more sales input to make sure the material they provide is good enough to cross the 'sophistication gap'.

> So it's the middle there between the sales machine and the marketing machine, which is where the majority of challenge exists.
>
> President, global high-tech

From the perspective of our global high-tech President it's in the middle of the marketing and sales machines where the challenge exists. This is another key reason to have absolute role clarity, particularly about what the hand-off point is so that we get the relay baton over the 'sophistication gap'. Clearly defining 'what good looks like' in relation to the state of the 'value proposition' material being passed over from marketing is key. Equally important is setting expectations for what sales needs to do in the 'last mile' towards the customer.

It's All About the Organisation—Or Is It?

We've heard some senior leaders come up with the simple diagnosis that all this misalignment can be sorted just by putting the two organisations under one head. Shame that life's just not that simple. In the words of Aretha Franklin, 'It ain't necessarily so'.

Or rather, in the words of one of our clients:

> I've also been on the other side where marketing was carved out and was a completely separate organisation reporting in directly through the CEO. And I think there are pros and cons to both approaches. I think, to answer your question, from an alignment standpoint marketing and sales reporting in to each other, that creates a strong and tight alignment. However, I would say what I noticed is it depends completely on the skillset of the person who's managing that organisation.
>
> Director of Marketing, US financial services company

They go on to say that if you have somebody who is a 100 % salesperson and they don't understand marketing, viewing it as only one little specific piece of the sales puzzle that was put on earth to serve sales, then alignment isn't created. That creates a lot of tension and unhappy employees on the marketing side, because they're not getting what they need.

> So yeah, I think that's it. I think it 100 % depends on the skills and ability of the person.
>
> Director of Marketing, US financial services company

By now we've said a number of times that the whole skillset issue is what we intend to cover in our next book. We wanted to acknowledge that we're aware of the view about organisation design. In the absence of any overwhelming evidence we take the view that separate organisations with aligned heads have a better chance of success than a unified organisation where the leader is myopic towards one of the functions.

Thought Worlds and Culture

> There are kind of cultural issues that salespeople and marketing people tend to have only worked in those areas for a period of time, they don't often move around, and they tend not to see the world from the other person's point of view.
>
> Vice-President of Sales Enablement, global corporation

At this point we feel we need to make a declaration. In case you hadn't noticed, we not only feel that this whole alignment thing is a big issue but we also hope we've presented enough evidence to prove it is. Before we complete this chapter we'll provide pragmatic advice on how to get aligned in order to execute the approach we're advocating for customer value in this book.

Overall, expecting you to solve this overnight is like hoping for world peace. In this space there are a number of issues you'll need to grapple with, and differing cultures and 'thought worlds' fall into this category.

For example our Vice-President of Sales Enablement friend is calling out a fairly common issue. The view that there's a cultural divide because staff don't move or swap roles often is one that can be seen in the academic literature today. Maybe you could use the programme advocated in this book to put in place some job swaps or some initiatives for working closer together. There seems to be plenty of scope for this given the results of our survey!

> How can you write a value proposition if you don't know what the problem is? And what I've also noticed is when we have a breakdown in maybe alignment is sometimes you'll have folk that are very, very smart, with a marketing mind, coming out of college but they only look smart. They don't know... They've never been in front of a real customer. They've never gone out even to Ted talks about things that are going on in the industry. And so because of that you get misalignment.
>
> Senior Vice-President, US-based global corporation

Again, falling into the resolution of world peace category we have the issue of thought world differences relating to education. Here we see that formal education versus real world experience can create misalignment. There are a number of issues here. The first sentence calls into question the ability of marketers to develop value propositions because they don't know what the customer's problems are. Our Senior Vice-President client seems to be advocating more customer contact. Quite often it's the sales organisation that acts as a barrier to these kinds of meetings taking place. They have to be prepared to facilitate these meetings or not get too upset if marketers set them up for themselves.

The 'formal' versus 'informal' education debate is a live one, as marketers are more likely to have formal academic qualifications. They need to be careful not to take these qualifications and nail them up in an ivory tower. What our client goes on to do is to suggest ways in how new marketers may be able to help.

> But you can get some new intelligence in regard to the latest things that are being studied maybe in college, some different ways to look at marketing where we might be a little bit outdated, so you get value but it's not the value that you may need to actually close that deal, it might be value to help us be more aware or try to differentiate ourselves in the market, but it's not something that is always going to drive that value proposition.
>
> Senior Vice-President, US-based global corporation

So, how well aligned marketing and sales are to the customer is an issue you need to be tackling regardless of whether you intend to implement the value proposition approach set out in our book. If clear expectations are set about respective roles and where value can be added this can move things forward. For example, we worked with one of our clients to help their marketing team to facilitate client workshops that were designed to help sales and to help the broader organisation gain a broader understanding of customer issues.

How Aligned Are Your Marketing and Sales to the Customer?

Having declared that achieving world peace is beyond the scope of this book,. we'll now introduce a model that brings together our view of all the commercial and academic research. Importantly, it's a tool you can use to assess where you currently are with suggestions on what you could do to get to the top right-hand corner 'Highway to heaven' box. This reflects our view that the most important facet is customer alignment, and that marketing and sales have to be aligned to make this work effectively.

After this, and recognising our inability to solve world peace, we'll provide pragmatic advice on how to get aligned in order to execute the programme suggested in this book (Fig. 9.4).

Road to Nowhere

Companies in this category think they're on a good path. Marketing and sales get along well and make an effort to produce a steady stream of content. The

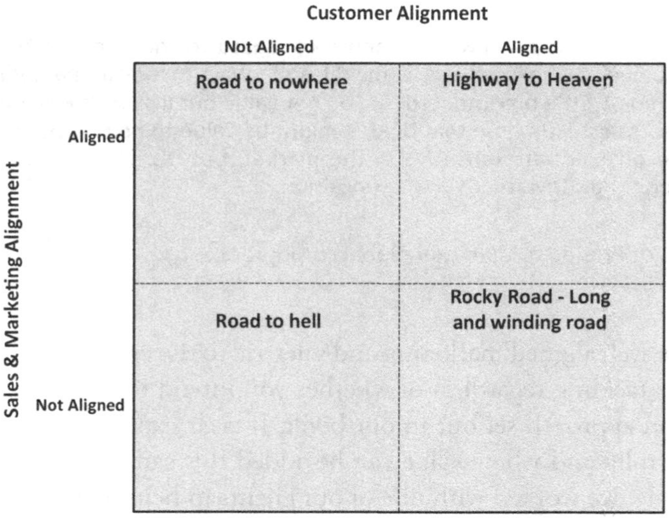

Fig. 9.4 Customer alignment roadmap

messaging is consistent and represents the brand well. The problem is that none of the content resonates with the customer. These firms haven't spent the time to truly understand what the customer really wants or needs before setting off on a path to create marketing materials. Marketing is likely to have a difficult time demonstrating the return on investment on any of their marketing tactics.

We advocate going back to Chap. 4 in this book, to spend more time and calories on customer research. After you've done this be sure to revisit all your customer-facing material. You may have a big effort ahead of you if you want to make it resonate with customers. At least you'll be empowered with lots of new intelligence about customer needs to help you craft true value propositions.

Road to Hell

Companies in this category have two major problems:

First, they do not really understand what motivates the customer. Marketing is likely to be producing marketing materials to appease the sales and product teams, and the messaging tends to be internally focused.

Second, marketing and sales are speaking different languages. Although both organisations aim to increase customer revenue, neither one fully understands how they can work together.

On this road to hell, marketing and sales could be wasting money on con-flicting messages and campaigns that confuse and overwhelm the customer.

Like the road to nowhere folks, you'll have to go back to Chap. 4 to spend more time and calories on understanding customers, markets and competi-tors. Given that the alignment problem could be a big issue, you should fol-low the steps we'll go through at the end of this chapter to execute against our programme.

We don't want to be all doom and gloom, but it's time to recognise that the longer you stay on this path, the more likely it is that your company won't survive. The implications of continuing to allow marketing and sales to work *against* each other, instead of *with* each other, is a high-stress, pressure-filled environment in which all of your best employees will eventually leave. Start to take steps to bridge the gap between the two departments. Are roles and responsibilities clearly outlined between the two groups? Do you have solid processes in place to handle customer inquiries and sales? Where are the breakdowns occurring?

And remember why you are in business in the first place—to serve your customers. Start by conducting customer research to determine what it's like to buy your products or services.

Rocky Road: Long and Winding Road

Companies in this category are operating in silos. Sales may be doing a great job conducting one-to-one customer conversations, collecting customer feed-back and adjusting their product offering accordingly. The problem is that this approach isn't scalable, and certainly not consistent in the customer's eyes.

In this world the customer may receive entirely different messages from your marketing channels as they do from your website or resource centre.

You can feel the tension inside your organisation. Sales and marketing are pointing fingers at each other as the 'reason' for not meeting revenue targets. Break down the barriers by bringing the focus back to the customer. Remember: you're both on the same side. Start by agreeing upon the ultimate goal you're trying to achieve. How can you break this into small steps or tasks to assign to either marketing or sales?

Let's look at it from your customer's point of view. How does a prospect become aware of your products and services? When they need help or a ques-tion answered during their decision-making process, how do they get the answers? When they raise their hand to speak to sales, how long does it take to get a call back? By putting yourself in the customer's shoes, you can stop pointing fingers internally and start addressing the breakdowns that may be occurring throughout their experience with your company.

Here we recommend you follow the steps to get aligned to the programme that are outlined in our book. There could be quite a few of you in this camp if you take into account what our surveys and depth interviews tell us.

Highway to Heaven

Companies in this category understand what motivates the customer. They commission regular research and harness sales feedback from customer interactions. This leads to the creation of relevant and worthy content, and a healthy working relationship between the marketing and sales organisations. From this platform they need to consistently use sales and marketing channels to drive growth.

It's no small task to be operating as smoothly as you are. To continue to stay in this quadrant, ensure that your marketing and sales teams are operating under a common set of shared metrics and goals. Review your progress frequently and dynamically adjust any areas that aren't working. Be especially mindful to apply the same practices when expanding your business into new product lines and/or territories.

The main danger of being in this box could be complacency. Remember what got you there today won't get you there tomorrow. We only have to look at the rise of non-asset-based companies such as Airbnb and Uber. Ask yourself if you're taking a broad enough scan of the environment to pick up potential developments like this. The question is what potential could we provide our customer that we don't currently? Exploring potential future value is the key here.

A Framework for Alignment

You should now have a clear view on where you sit on the customer alignment roadmap. We hope you found our tips for improving alignment helpful in starting you on a path for improvement. We'll conclude this chapter by providing some pragmatic tips and templates on how to get aligned in order to execute the value-based approach outlined in this book. These will help you 'unlock customer value' and drive growth.

Before we do this, we feel it's important to draw together what we know so far about sales and marketing alignment towards the customer. We hope you'll find this useful, as regardless of whether you intend to execute the programme we suggest there are some fundamental principles for alignment you should address before you embark on the road to unlocking customer value; towards value-ology. These themes should be no surprise to you as they come out of a thematic analysis of the academic and commercial, and our own primary research. These are laid out in Fig. 9.5.

If you follow our GRRIPS alignment framework you should be in a good position to kick off the value-ology programme, as you'll have begun to get a 'GRRIPS' on this thorny issue.

Goal Alignment

We've seen that getting this right is key to driving towards alignment. Here we recommend that the 'strategic goals' need to look the same as the scorecards of the Chief Marketing Officer (CMO) and the President of Sales. These need to go as far down the organisation as possible, we can't see a good reason why they shouldn't go all the way down through sales and marketing organisations. We define 'strategic goals' as those that have to be achieved for the organisation to thrive and survive: revenue, sales, profitability, customer satisfaction and market share.

Underpinning these should be tactical goals that relate to how certain roles contribute towards the overall strategic goals. For example, a marketing communications manager may have a goal to raise awareness about the company and its offer. A campaign manager may have a goal to generate a certain num-

Theme	Action
Goals	Set common 'strategic goals' for marketing and sales (see Fig. 9.8). Integrate tactical goals that compliment strategic goals.
Roles	Understand that roles and interlocking and must work in harmony to achieve success. Agree 'duties' and 'rights' (see Fig. 9.4)
Resources	Ensure resources required to 'get the job done' are understood. Develop clear mechanisms for budget requests and allocation.
Information and conversation flow	To be aligned to the customer there needs to be a constant flow back from the market place. Agree information flow and process for coordination.
Processes	Agree key processes for moving towards goals.
Success Measures	Agree what success looks like. Measure against the strategic goals. Make sure top level score cards are all the same colour!

Fig. 9.5 GRRIPS alignment framework

ber of leads to 'feed' the sales force. A sales manager may have a goal to turn round leads within a certain length of time. These tactical goals have to 'roll-up' towards the strategic goals.

Reward should be linked to strategic goals at all levels. The percentage of remuneration tied to tactical goals will vary at different levels and roles in the organisation.

Role Alignment

There has to be an understanding that the marketing and sales roles are inter-locking and must work in harmony for the strategic goals to be achieved. We will come to this one final time, when we specifically discuss roles relating to the 'sophistication gap' that needs to be crossed in order to develop relevant customer value propositions. Use the template we provided in Fig. 9.4 to agree on a core set of 'duties' and 'rights'.

Resources

These can be financial, physical or human resources. We have already seen that there can be tension around the need for more marketing spend ver-sus more 'feet on the street' account managers. Developing a mechanism for jointly sharing the 'asks' for more resource is a difficult but a good place to get to.

Coming to a joint understanding of what marketing and sales need to do together to deliver for the customer is key here. This isn't something that can be easily done on a template, though maybe a facilitated workshop can help.

Information and Conversation Flow

From our standpoint, what good looks like here is that marketing and sales conversations are dominated by customer value. What we mean is that sales provides input from the hundreds of customer meetings they attend, which add to direct input that marketing gets from customers through more formal research. Marketing then makes sense of all the input and uses it to reshape buyer personas, communications, products and value propositions. The responsibilities for providing this input can be captured within the duties and rights exercise as part of role alignment. The Customer Alignment Map questionnaire should have helped you form a view of what the customer–sales–marketing information flow is like, and should have given you some tips for improvement.

The next useful step could be to write down your current information and conversation flow practices and compare them with your desired state. This should generate a set of actions to help you bridge the gap. For example, marketing might currently request competitor intelligence from sales infrequently and informally. This may mean you don't have a good handle on what your competitors are doing. Getting to a point where this is done more systematically and frequently could be helpful here.

Processes

Agreeing the top five processes that need to be developed for effective alignment could be a great starting point here. Once this has been done these processes can be mapped out with clear roles and responsibilities. We saw earlier that in the campaign process it's helpful to have clear definitions for what makes a good lead along with a clear process for passing leads to sales. The duties and rights exercise should have taken care of sales' 'right' to expect good leads and their duty to follow up on leads passed from marketing within a specified period of time.

Success

Defining what success looks like will help you set strategic goals and drive them down into both marketing and sales organisations. What has to happen is that measurement of performance reflects this, as does reward. We have to make sure that we don't have the situation we found earlier, where sales scorecards were red and marketing scorecards were green. This can be avoided if strategic goals are aligned.

A sense of shared reward can be usefully nurtured here. If all the strategic goals are green, there has to be a mechanism for ensuring all marketing and salespeople feel the benefit of this.

And Finally ... Alignment for Value-Ology

We are not intentionally avoiding the culture and thought world aspect. This merits a whole separate discussion as we are grappling with a big issue here. Coming to terms with the complex set of values and beliefs that define the way in which a firm conducts its business is a simple definition of culture which outlines its complexity. This has to be a constant source of discussion around the marketing and sales table. Here we suggest some pragmatic steps that fall within our 'unlocking customer value' approach. We will unashamedly be following the flow of the book.

The first two steps relate to a culturally problematic issue: language.

Alignment for Value-Ology

Steps 1 and 2 Mind Your Language!

The first two chapters were devoted to value and value propositions. Hopefully we demonstrated that these are words with highly contested meanings. Having got to GRRIPS with key alignment issues the first thing you need to do is to agree on the definitions you will use and share for value and value propositions.

> Definition of value = Perceived relevant and distinct benefit − Total cost of ownership

You should be familiar with this definition as we presented it in Chap. 1. Get the key players from marketing and sales to discuss and agree a definition of value that works for your organisation. Some customer input may be useful here too. While you're at it you may want to do the same for value propositions. We present the same template for defining value propositions as we did in Chap. 2 at the end of this chapter for you to complete this step.

Step 3 What Does Marketing Need to Provide to Sales to Allow Them to Confidently Develop Value in a Social Setting?

In Chap. 3 we highlighted our research into developing value in the social setting involving the customer and the salesperson.

To enable the salesperson to thrive in this environment we feel it's useful to have a clear understanding of what marketing needs to give them, to help them concentrate on social value. If you're a marketer, why not ask them?

What's clear from all the research is that sales is being carpet-bombed with all manner of marketing 'content' that they don't use. Often they spend time re-working what's provided for them because it doesn't hit the mark. Over recent weeks we've had two contrasting conversations. A Head of Marketing for a global IT company gave us a huge laundry list of 'stuff' they provide for sales. When asked which they found most useful we were invited to 'go and ask sales!'. A more enlightened Vice-President of Marketing at another global organisation focused on two or three key outputs that sales said they valued.

We expect that sales will want:

- A clear view of your overall company value proposition. One that is focused on customer value.
- Key value themes to hang conversations around
- Some insight into the issues faced by the customers in the industry they serve
- Key points of difference between you and the competition
- Case studies on where you've done this before

If they have this clarity they won't be left floundering if the customer presses them on what your company does to add customer value.

Step 4 Enhancing Market and Customer Understanding

The templates we suggested earlier in relation to information flows may be helpful. Here we return to the 'soap-bar' value proposition stack model we introduced in Chap. 2 and amended in Fig. 9.5 to include the 'sophistication gap'.

Marketing definitely needs to do the bulk of the work at the bottom of the stack to get an understanding of key customer issues and suggest key proposition themes. Moving towards the top of the stack the need for sales input becomes stronger. At customer industry level, it may be that sales has spent years serving the same sector, such as financial services. Their input should be key in helping to shape the industry vertical value proposition.

We've seen from our earlier research that salespeople often find what they get from marketing 'too generic' as the dialogue moves towards the customer. Here there has to be absolute clarity about who does what to transform industry-level propositions into those that resonate with individual members of buying units with a particular customer. Sales have to play a prominent role in crafting relevant and resonant material based on quality groundwork provided by marketing. By definition this is likely to be more resonant with sales if they were involved towards the bottom of the stack.

This goes hand in hand with clarity of roles and processes around information. Completing the template at Fig. 9.9 will help provide a platform for more formally recording how to keep on top of customers and competitors.

Step 5 Campaign Alignment

We've already touched on the need for campaign alignment in Chap. 7. To summarise, we feel there needs to be alignment on:

Language: What Do We Mean by Campaign?

This can be a problem between the different marketing camps as well as with sales. It's probably worth reminding ourselves about the overall philosophy of our approach to get to a definition. Let's start by putting ourselves in the customer's shoes.

A customer of an organisation who deals with life on a product-by-product basis will soon 'tune out' of your campaigns if you hit them every time you have something you want to say about an individual problem. This was the problem we faced at BT and something a Sales Senior Vice-President of a global company was bemoaning yesterday. You can go from hundreds of products to one or two campaigns by selecting 'themes' that you campaign under. In this brave new world the customer isn't bombarded and all the content they get is linked to an issue they should feel is relevant; for example, 'Agility', 'Growth' or 'Productivity'. After all, the themes came from customer research!

Goals and Roles: Again!

You should have begun to fix this from the earlier GRRIPS exercise. You need to revisit these to agree campaign-level goals that aggregate back up to overall strategic goals. Agreeing an overall campaign objective is useful here before agreeing joint revenue, sales and customer satisfaction. Make sure that these campaign goals are reflected in the pay and reward plans for both marketing and sales, or you're fighting an uphill battle.

Agree clear roles between marketing and sales in respect of campaign launch, training and coaching. If the organisation sees marketing and sales standing together to launch campaigns, this will dramatically enhance buy-in.

Clearly define what a good lead looks like before agreeing a process for lead hand-off and follow up. Make sure you have agreement on what the success measures are, and are clear on what is going to be reported and how. We've seen many a good campaign fall down because of over-reporting sales as attributable to the campaign.

Step 6 Alignment for Account Based Marketing (ABM)

We explored this reasonably new phenomenon (or is it?) in Chap. 8. Organisations that exclusively offer ABM tools will often say improved alignment is achieved as well as uplift in sales. We would take the view that it helps if the GRRIPS groundwork has already taken place before you go into an ABM programme.

All the recommendations we've made for getting alignment to effectively execute for 'unlocking customer value' hold true for ABM. Marketing and sales goals and roles become more granular as you deal with one or a few accounts. Getting clarity on lead follow-up becomes more crucial here as it's likely to be an important customer that you're affecting.

It Sounds Simple ... but It Ain't Easy
Hopefully we've drawn out a few of the big issues around marketing and sales alignment to customer needs. Like all relationships, nurturing and developing them sounds simple ... but it ain't easy. If you've followed the flow you should now have a plan to improve the alignment to put you in the 'Stairway to Heaven' box. In this box you'll understand your customers' needs clearly so that your value propositions resonate and drive growth for both your business and your customer.

And so, to conclude...

Further Reading

Beverland, M., Steel, M. G., & Dapiran, P. (2006). *Cultural frames that drive sales and marketing apart: An exploratory study. Journal of Business and Industrial Marketing, 21*(6), 386–394.

Cespedes, F. V. (1996). *Beyond teamwork: How the wise can synchronize. Marketing Management, 5*(1), 25–37.

Cespedes, F. V. (2014). *Aligning strategy and sales: The choices, systems and behaviors that drive effective selling.* Boston: Harvard Business Review Press.

Donath, B. (1999, September 13). Get marketing, sales on same wavelength. *Marketing News,*)p. 16.

Homburg, C., & Jensen, O. (2007). *The thought worlds of marketing and sales: Which differences make a difference? Journal of Marketing, 71,* 124–142.

Homburg, C., Jensen, O., & Krohmer, H. (2008). *Configurations of marketing and sales: A taxonomy. Journal of Marketing, 72*(2), 133–154.

Kotler, P., Rackham, N., & Kirshnaswamy, S. (2007). *Ending the war between sales and marketing. Harvard Business Review on Strategic Sales Management,* 23–48.

Malshe, A., & Sohi, R. S. (2009). *Sales buy-in of marketing strategies: Exploration of its nuances, antecedents and contextual conditions. Journal of Personal Selling and Sales Management, 29*(3), 207–225.

Panigyrakis, G. G., & Veloutsu, C. A. (1999). *Brand managers' interfaces in different consumer goods industries. Journal of Product & Brand Management, 8*(1), 19–37.

Pisello, T. (2015b). *Frugalnomics survival guide: How to use your unique value to market better, stand out and sell more.* Winter Park: Alinean Press.

Randstad research. (2015). Do you have siloed operations? Sales and Marketing- the missing link https://www.randstad.co.uk/employers/sales-marketing-alignment-report/. Accessed 23 Nov 2016.

Rouziès, D., & Hulland, J. (2014). *Does marketing and sales integration always pay off? Evidence from a social capital perspective. Journal of the Academy of Marketing Science, 42*(5), 511–527.

Sirius Decisions Research. (2014). Four critical areas of marketing and sales operations alignment. https://www.siriusdecisions.com/Blog/2014/Dec/Four-Critical-Areas-of-Marketing-and-Sales-Operations-Alignment. Accessed 23 Nov 2016.

Strahle, W. M., Spiro, R. L., & Acito, F. (1996). *Marketing and sales: Strategic alignment and functional implementation. Journal of Personal Selling and Sales Management, 16*(Winter), 1–20.

Workman Jr., J. J., Homburg, C., & Gruner, K. (1998). Marketing organization: An integrative framework of dimensions and determinants. *Journal of Marketing, 62*(3), 21–41.

Yandle, J., & Blythe, J. (2000). *Intra-departmental conflict between sales and marketing: An exploratory study. Journal of Selling and Major Account Management, 2*(3), 3–31.

10

Cohesion Is the New Differentiator: Are You Ready?

Congratulations: you've almost got to the end of our book. We hope you've enjoyed it so far and more importantly that you've begun to move the customer value approach forward in your organisation. Right now you're probably wondering whether to bother reading these concluding remarks; we've been there.

Pardon the pun (please stick with it), the moral of the story is that cohesion is the new differentiator, the new point of competitive advantage: Cohesive Advantage. So what is it?

Cohesion is the act or state of creating unity or sticking together. This book has been all about cohering to customer value and maintaining that cohesion through your marketing and sales teams. In this approach, customer value is the hero, not your products. You and your company are the guide or mentor unlocking the door to show them how you can help them realise value and achieve their business goals. Your conversations are now centred on customer value themes that give you a much more powerful platform to communicate what your solutions can do for the customer. In this omni-channel world you can achieve cohesion through a mix of online and offline tactics. You can demonstrate you seek to answer critical questions for customers and leave them in no doubt about how well your firm understands what they value and how you can help them.

From the organisation's perspective, cohesion is attained by understanding your customers so well that you are able to lead them, in a frictionless way, to a solution that only you can provide; by uniting sales and marketing in the delivery of value at each stage of your customer's journey.

© The Author(s) 2017
S. Kelly et al., *Value-ology*,
DOI 10.1007/978-3-319-45626-3_10

In Chap. 9 we gave you some tools to test for alignment. The aim is to get your organisation into the 'Highway to Heaven' box, which is a state of cohesion. In this state there's a great interaction between the customer and your marketing and sales teams. If you're in this box you'll have got great processes in place for understanding customer value and developing compelling value propositions. Crucially, you'll have found a way to make sense of the daily conversations your sales teams are having with customers. You'll be using this to inform changes you may need to make to your approach on the basis of what you're hearing out in the market. If you're in this box for marketing and sales alignment with the customer you might want to get your customer service function aligned. After all, we agree with Vargo and Lusch, and their Service Dominant Logic, that value is only truly experienced when a customer starts to consume your solutions 'in use'.

We have a pretty straightforward model to describe this, which we call the Cohesive Loop (Fig. 10.1). This recognises that although the vision, mission, strategy and value proposition may have come from the marketing function nothing has really happened until dialogue with the customer starts. In a world where you have Cohesive Advantage, marketing will have had the good sense to engage customers and sales in helping to shape these. If you've done this then there's likely to be better buy-in from sales as you take your value propositions back out to the market. The customer should recognise the value you're promising to deliver as value because you based your propositions on what they told you was important. This model is a continuous loop, taking feedback from the field in the shape of customers, sales and ultimately servicepeople.

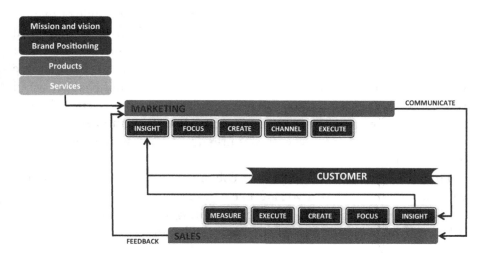

Fig. 10.1 The Cohesive Loop

Chris Argyris (1999) said that many companies are single loop learners who focus on identifying and correcting errors in the environment that is external to themselves. This could be fixing a price point, making a channel decision, creating a new brand identity, changing the way other departments work. In reality, organisations should become double loop learners who take a candid look at themselves and critically reflect on their own thinking and behaviour and how that affects performance. Argyris says:

> whenever single loop strategies go wrong people screen out criticism and put the blame on anyone but themselves

We think our Cohesive Loop takes on board the principles of double loop learning. In fact, we would say that it goes beyond this by creating an integrated system for learning which is continuous. You could call this a Perpetual Learning Cycle moving around a virtuous circle, which is the Cohesive Loop.

We acknowledge that in an immature state there could be some semblance of dialogue between the customer, sales and marketing that is really 'single loop'. We took this into account in the questions we built into our 'alignment-ometer'. You can only land in the 'Highway to Heaven' box if the dialogue is strategic and not just very tactical. If your conversations are just about marketing tactics not working, sales not executing against leads, the need for more marketing events, you're not standing back and 'double loop learning'. So we only view a Cohesive Loop as working optimally if there's a virtuous learning cycle, not finger pointing to detract from your own performance.

If you're well on the way to developing a Cohesive Advantage you'll have a mechanism for perpetually learning about the market and macro environment. This will help you avoid becoming the next Boston Ice company, which fails to notice changes in technology that alter how value is delivered in your market. You could become the next Airbnb or Uber, and find new ways to create customer value.

So what happens if you don't do what we're advocating in this book? If you've read this far it's unlikely that you'll fall into this trap. If you haven't or don't intend to move to the customer value based model we suggest you go back and re-read the introduction, because that's where you'll be, back at the start.

We know that today 52 % of the companies listed in Fortune 500 in 2000 are no longer on the list. Without competitively differentiated and resonating value propositions your firm will die. Without alignment between sales, marketing and the customer your firm will die. Bob Garrat, in his book *The*

Fish Rots from the Head, describes the death of a company that fails to learn about markets, customers and itself as 'often slow and Grisly'.

As we have seen, marketing and sales exist as two functions in larger firms, quite understandably for resource and management reasons. That said, despite working for the same firm or brand they can often see the world differently and think about it in different ways.

Sales and marketing see themselves as *related* but not necessarily *aligned*. This means they frequently regard each other as separate entities, with one treating the other as 'external' to itself. When the sales graph takes a dip, sales often sees marketing as the problem and marketing sees sales as the problem. When they think like this they're thinking in what Argyris calls a single loop way. Each function sees the solution to the problem of alignment as anywhere but in their own backyard.

If you've decided to do nothing this is the world you've elected to continue to inhabit. Good luck with that: it may not be for long!

This may be uncharitable, as your company may be in a more advanced state than this. Hopefully that's because you've acted on some of the things we've discussed (Fig. 10.2).

Exercise 10.1
So where do you think you sit on our value proposition maturity model? Discuss this with your colleagues. If you've taken action from the time you first opened this book it might be interesting to think about where you started and where you are now.

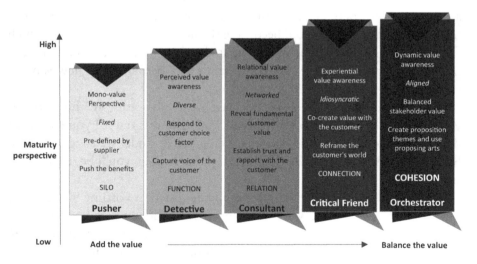

Fig. 10.2 Value proposition maturity model

An organisation at the extreme left is what Jill Konrath in *Agile Selling* (2015) calls 'Product Peddlers'. We prefer to call them 'Pushers' because of the negative connotation that word has. At this end of the spectrum companies 'push' their wares on unwitting customers. This is OK if you're the fake perfume seller outside the Blue Mosque in Istanbul because your 'customer' is unlikely to see you again. In business to business, if you're looking to develop sales over a sustained period of time, it's not where you want to be. If you manage to hoodwink the customer into buying something, he'll exact revenge next time you try.

If you're the rare breed that finds itself at the far right of the spectrum you're a value-orchestrator. Here your organisation is in the 'Highway to Heaven' box as it relates to our cohesion model. You have great alignment between customer, sales and marketing. You're seen by the customer as an organisation that proactively proposes new ways to help them realise business value. It's highly likely that you're viewed as a partner who's interested in helping the customer move the needle on their business results. You happen to sell lots of solutions to them as a consequence of understanding, articulating and helping them realise value—your value-ology.

By the time you've landed on the far right of the spectrum you'll have moved through the phases implied in this statement from Lusch and Webster:

> Strategy formulation is essentially a process of matching the networked firm's competencies and capabilities with customer needs and preferences, identifying latent customer demand that is relatively underserved by competitors' value propositions.

They go on to say that 'bad' potential customers are those who do not value the firm's resources and capabilities and are therefore unwilling to provide reciprocal resources or service in their interactions with the marketer enterprise.

This helps explain why we view customer value as the hero as it is not customer worship. There has to be mutual value in the process we've described that helps enhance the bottom line for both your customer and you. In fact, you don't have to be at the far right of the spectrum to have jettisoned the 'bad' customers. Only yesterday we were speaking to a client who's just about to embark on this journey. He told us about a 'segment' of customers that beats him up on price, asks for the world, is difficult to deal with and gives nothing back. So why bother? You can make the decision not to serve these early on in your journey along the spectrum and feel the joy of a quick win.

To the Future: A Word on Skills—Another Elephant in the Room?

We have seen that value is anything but a purely objective thing that can be analysed and quantified. We have also seen how people interpret what value means in different ways and that there is skill in subjectively interpreting what they mean when they refer to value. It is clear, therefore, that sales and marketing practice is a blend of the objective and subjective—value-ology.

On the one hand, there's the detailed objective commercial analysis of business plans and campaigns, and on the other the emotional understanding that is needed for creating powerful brand associations. One day professionals are concerned with a structured and logical approach to account management and the next with interpersonal and social skills of face-to-face interactions. The deep capability of sales and marketing professionals is the ability to successfully balance and orchestrate objectivity and subjectivity.

Being objective is nevertheless believed to be the gold standard of business effectiveness. By acting in a rational and objective way it is taken as evidence that you're cool headed, shrewd and calculated. The really interesting thing, though, is that when you get sales and marketing professionals talking off the record about what makes them stand out from their competitors, it's the subjective things that make the difference.

So what does this tell us? Well, going right back to the beginning, it explains why we didn't want to produce one of those books that you can open in order to instantly 'crowd storm' your value propositions.

A big advocate of this customer value-led approach is an old colleague, Tony Kane. He's sold successfully for several of the world's leading blue chip ICT companies using this approach and holds the view, as we do, that:

> A value proposition is the difference between the value you can provide and the cost of the thing you are providing

His rider to this is profound, or we think so:

> Getting the costs is easy, understanding and articulating value is not

Salespeople tend to get lots of 'value-ology' training with high-quality organisations to help them try to unearth value from customer conversations and present value to customers. With all this we've seen that they have difficulty articulating value as far as customers are concerned. Qvidian research says that

58 % of deals end up in 'no decision' because sales has not presented value effectively.

What we've presented in value-ology is a process and a set of tools to help you move to a point where you can become a 'value orchestrator'. Hopefully we've outlined some of the challenges and pitfalls on the way through, with some tools to help you avoid them.

We recognise that this book doesn't tackle some of the skill set issues that we believe need to be recruited, trained and coached. Earlier this week we met a former first class marketing graduate from a client of ours who acknowledges the problem we're alluding to here. Marketers tend to be classically trained on the core concepts of marketing or are provided with the technical competencies. However, we don't believe this is what will make a difference between successful and unsuccessful implementation of our approach. There's a long list of different skills required throughout this process:

- The left brain analytical skills to be able to analyse data about markets and customers
- Right brain creativity, which starts early in the process to help unearth customer value that may have not been seen before
- Lots of soft skills that are too numerous to mention: the ability to get stakeholder buy-in from sales and senior executives, negotiation skills, resilience, etc.

There's certainly scope for a follow-up work on 'value-ology mastery', which could look at the skills required to unlock customer value.

Finally ... This Is Not an Option

Hopefully you've begun the journey towards a more customer value-based approach and are starting to feel the excitement and reap some benefits. We don't see that there is another option unless you want to wither on the vine with other product pushers. Organisations that are failing to understand customer value are failing to get their attention. In fact 94 % of them have disengaged with organisations like yours because you've been sending them irrelevant rubbish. If you're doing this you're wasting 94 % of the money you're spending on 'content' and losing customers by the day.

Cohesion is the new differentiator. Cohesive Advantage is the new competitive advantage. If you can get your marketing and sales teams aligned to customers and what they value you'll be ahead of the pack. If you can connect the dots for customers to demonstrate that you understand their issues and deliver value for them you become one of the 6 % of organisations whose 'content' doesn't get consigned to the electronic waste bin.

If you don't do this now you'll continue to be noise to the customer, and will whimper to an untimely death that nobody will hear. Walk towards the sunny uplands, be the organisation that gets its content share because it resonates with customers. Remember that 91 % of your customers will do this for you if their value relevance buttons are pressed.

So, what's it to be: 10 % plus revenue and profitability growth or constant price battles leading to a 16 % annual decline in profit? Make the choice, if you still feel there is one.

Further Reading

Argyris, C. (1999). *On organisational learning* (2nd ed.). London: Wiley-Blackwell.
Konrath, J. (2014). *Agile selling: Get up to speed quickly in today's ever-changing sales world*. New York: Penguin.

Glossary

Ansoff's matrix an analysis framework that defines the strategic direction possibilities for a business

Five Forces an analysis framework of competitive forces created by Michael Porter, comprising power of suppliers, power of buyers, threat of substitutes, threat of new entrants and industry rivalry

PEST analysis a framework of the business environment analysing Political, Economic, Social and Technological factors

Positioning the competitive position a business seeks to take in a market, also referring to how people perceive a brand

Segmentation the categorisation of customer types by aspects of similarity

SWOT analysis an analysis framework of business factors affecting a business, namely Strengths, Weaknesses, Opportunities and Threats

Targeting a selection process that prioritises the focus of customer-related activities against a specific customer segment or segments

© The Author(s) 2017
S. Kelly et al., *Value-ology*,
DOI 10.1007/978-3-319-45626-3

Index

Note: Page number followed by 'n' refers to notes.

© The Author(s) 2017
S. Kelly et al., *Value-ology*,
DOI 10.1007/978-3-319-45626-3

9783319456256